16 Minutes

When One Breath Ends, Another Begins

16 Minutes

When One Breath Ends, Another Begins

Roland M. Comtois

Published by Chalice Communications, LLC
East Killingly, Connecticut
www.chalicecommunications.com

Copyright © 2013 Roland M. Comtois

www.rolandcomtois.net

Cover design by Roland M. Comtois

Book design by John Catlin & Roland M. Comtois

Editorial by Cindy Clarke

Printed in the United States of America

First Printing: June 2013

ISBN # 978-0-9824536-1-2

Library of Congress Control Number: 2013910800

Table of Contents

Dedication

"Mom, I love you with every part of my heart."

Theresa M. Comtois

From My Heart to Yours . . .

To my daughter, Kaitlin Comtois, who showed amazing courage during her own time of grief, thanks for sharing grandma's story with me. You are my heart and soul. And, thanks for letting me cry. Thank you to Timothy Morvan, for all of your loving support during my time of need. To my sister, Lori-Ann Ethier, we were blessed to have Mom for as long as we did. She was our life and we were hers. To Russell Ethier, thank you for being there for Mom. To Bradford, Isaiah, Bethany, Rebekah, Malaki, Brooke and Shannon, Grandma, loved you guys so much.

To all those who have walked this journey with me, thank you for allowing me to share my story with you, I deeply thank you: Patricia Pepler, Kathy St. Germain, Tina Bottecelli, Debbie Grenon, Linda Hogan, Lisa Bonnell, Carrie Butts, Dawn Penta, Kathy Imondi, Diane Lupo, Steve Lupo, Nancy Cingari, Chip Cingari, Tracy Mignone, and June Fagan.

To Cindy Clarke, Barb Conetta, JoAnn Wolff and Susan L. Arel-Comtois, I am indebted to you for your honest and sincere review of my book. Words cannot express the depth of my gratitude for your care and nurturing of my sacred words. Thank you for reading every single word.

To the amazing staff at Friendly Home, Woonsocket, RI, thank you for dedication, care and loving support of my mother.

To the many people who walk the difficult journey of grief, please know that you are not alone. I am there with you.

Foreword

I've spent nearly a lifetime exposing the spiritual truth that heaven exists. From my visit with my departed grandmother three days after she passed away forty years ago, to my near-death experience some twenty years later, had life-altering experiences that formed my perspective about heaven and the after-life. I remember in both instances a glowing, warm, nurturing light showing me that there is more beyond here, more than what we can possibly imagine. I saw my grandmother's eyes, the angel's wings and felt safe. I witnessed heaven's beauty and felt its breathtaking love from the second I departed this life for a rare glimpse of heaven to the moment of my first new breath back on Earth.

In my work I offer the possibility of endless and infinite connections that occurs between two people who truly love each other. My understanding, which is profoundly entrenched within the core of my being, is that there is life beyond physical death.

Story after story proclaiming that love lives on and what we meant to each other still exists deep within the soul of the person who has passed away continues to inspire me. Religious stories, told throughout the centuries, denoting that one has risen and one lives gives me hope that this life is simply the beginning of our exploration. Sacred channeled messages and spiritual signs demonstrate that the one who has passed remains on the continuum of love long after they leave this place and this gives me strength.

Eternal love cannot be tainted, nor stilled by death. I've sat with mothers who have lost children, and children who have lost fathers, but absolutely nothing has prepared me for the loss of my mother.

As I stand at the threshold of my mother's passing, would my years of faith make the experience of losing her easier? Would my knowledge of God, angels and all of the spiritual entities that bring love from beyond make this process more comfortable for me? Would my belief in eternal love, sacred channeled messages, signs from heaven, make dealing with the loss of my mother easier? No! Loss hurts no matter who you are, what you know or where you come from. Loss involves the physical bond that we share with each other. One hand holding another, a mother kissing her child, a father sharing a moment with his son, a warm embrace from friend to friend and the opportunity to look into someone's eyes suggest that you are alive and living in the power of one singular moment.

As I experience the last days of my mother's life, I will attempt to hold close to my heart my deep truth . . . that love is eternal.

Prologue

It's so true that no one can prepare you for the event of losing someone so dear. The knowledge one has about the physical body and its inability to survive the longevity of life holds no merit to the experience of loss. The faithfulness that one has collected over the years acknowledging that some higher power exists doesn't wash away the deep sadness that arises at the loss of a loved one. The clarity one feels about the after-life, knowing that love is everlasting, does not alter the despair that one feels at the moment grief knocks on the door.

What loss does is force you to pause, to put your life on hold, to re-evaluate who you are and to challenge every ounce of faithfulness inside of you. Grief then materializes into a transitory moment of fear, the yearning to be together is scorched into your mind, and mountains of questions become part of your essence.

In my wildest dreams I would never have imagined the intensity of physical pain as I now experience it on a deep and personal level. My heart aches, my stomach hurts and my soul bleeds, but what can you really do? Losing someone to death creates an itinerary of encounters and questions that seem to saturate your thinking. Sometimes it's guilt you feel and other times it's hope and the thought of their passing remains a constant component of our thinking.

I know about pain that is related to the loss of loved ones, but not like this. Some have said there seems to be a difference in the depth of loss depending on who passes, but judgment and comparison cannot and should not exist. When your mother dies, it's excruciating. When you dad dies, it hurts immeasurably, and when your grandmother, friend or even a beloved pet passes, you feel such loss. What you feel is what you feel, no matter who passes away! Grief, in the end, will take you to the threshold of a new path that must be visited. How to walk that path and what is best for you, personally, will be discovered as you place your foot on the walkway of your life.

Despite my need for time to stand still, it would not. In my attempts to stop my future from becoming my present nothing was in my control anymore. Or was it? Now, I just have to walk one step at a time, breathe as peacefully as I can and start over again every time I am reminded that my mother is gone.

Every human being experiences loss and each of us feel it so differently. Some have moved forward, and others have stood still, not dependent on one thing or another, but many things I'm sure. "Time heals all wounds" has been an expression to offer someone grief support at a time of need, but I've discovered that time does nothing at all. Love heals the wounds or at least it does for me. When I remember the love my Mom and I shared, it seems to ease the aches and pains of grief even for a brief moment, and the numbness that penetrates my being temporarily floats away somewhere.

Time gives you moments to adjust to a new way of living. It offers you "time" to stretch your broken heart into the healing light of love and stitches together the pieces of your soul that shattered when your loved one passed. Time tells you that life is so different now, and offers you moments to remember the love. It doesn't laugh at you, nor does it mock you. It's simply there to assist you towards your healing.

This story is about the last sixteen minutes shared between mother and son, about the sixteen minutes that followed her passing, about grief, healing, time, spiritual messages, and celebration. It is also about the life lessons that my new teacher, grief, has taught me.

It is my intention that you find, tucked within the words of this story, hope and the possibility that love shared is endless and that when one breath ends, another begins.

God is in here.

Spirit is in here.

Love is in here.

And they are all one and the same.

One

One Moment Before the Next

One hour spills into another and time seems to hold my breath hostage. I sit quietly, barely peaceful, as I have for the last thirty hours of her final journey from this physical material world to her spiritual place. I pray, desperately, for a whimper or a whisper of my name, but her voice lay in a silent tomb somewhere far beyond time. We've spent the last night together with my head nestled upon her shoulder, me, stroking her arm and she, breathing effortlessly for the first time in a long time. The only thing I could offer her was my unbridled love and somehow that was enough. The moments we shared during the night are now a timeless, priceless heirloom that I carry in my heart.

I keep within arm's reach my grief so not to disturb the journey that she must take, but I want to scream out in agony. My body cries out with insufferable uncontrollable pain and my mind cannot comprehend life without her. I imagine if she really knew how broken hearted I felt that she might delay her passage to the next place. I want not to confuse this moment with my personal need, but to go beyond myself and support my mother to achieve her greatest desire—to finally be free from her pain. I, too, want to erase from my mind the suffering that I've witnessed for years and want to rejoice in the fact that soon she will be free from the physical limitation that has held her for so long. All I can really do is saturate this moment with as much love as I can, for her and for me, too.

The night is long. Mom lays sleeping, cocooned in the white sheets and pink bedspread that she carried from home. Remnants of her apartment are scattered throughout her two-by-four living space and her favorite newly reupholstered rocking chair sits vacant in the corner of her room. Each minute that passes by I immerse myself in the love that we shared together, hopeful that it will carry me to the next second. Life memories showcased in my mind seem to play out like a home video. I remember the good times, loving times and challenging times too, but all are a part the whole story. It becomes very evident to me that without these stories I wouldn't be sitting here. I am thankful for each and every one of them for they have made me the man I am.

Time slips away, and soon on this November day the sun will rise up into the blue skies. I see from my seat a glimmer of light shining through the bedroom shade. The quietness and darkness that filled the night begins to find its pulse. This is a new day, one I will never forget. Is this really her final day? The trees seem to dance in the wind, somehow beckoning her home to be where she finally wants to be. The hurriedness of living is no more and the worries about how to live life will evaporate as the morning emerges into afternoon.

I wonder what the next moment will bring as each breath becomes a tribute to a life lived. In my mind I imagine heaven's gate welcoming her home, just like the family gatherings so long ago. You know that feeling when you walk into a room and everyone is glad to see you? They shout your name and glee decorates their faces with joy. I know that they will greet her and take care of her for me, and I will begin my destination towards grief, sorrow and learning to live my new normal life. The one person, my Mom, who has known me from beyond the beginning, is now easing into her eternity.

Two

Two Days Before the New Day Dawns

The bandage that covered her left arm remained intact, legs swollen three times their size, and she, adorned in her favorite red sweatshirt, glowed with an uncanny peacefulness that seemed to surprise me. Words of wisdom echo in the small nursing home room that had become her refuge for the last eight weeks. Her smile was grander and brighter than the day before and a glint of light grew from her eyes, like that of a blossom finding the sun. She spoke with an ease in her voice, like she had spontaneously become a guru. She has much to tell me, she says, before the final day is upon us. Her voice is slightly edgy sparked by enthusiasm and anchored in courage. She was beginning to find her strength.

She leaned forward to whisper, to share her words. I thought she'd say as she did a thousand times before that she wanted to "go," that living had become a constant struggle of fighting the internal persecution and debilitating diseases. Mom's last years of life were a constant vigil of trying to fight the fear and the pain of life, living and dying. She fought valiantly, one condition after another, and it took its toll on her. Now, somehow through the mystery of it all, she is beginning her ascension to another dwelling place, somewhere over the rainbow.

As she began to speak her face became illuminated and glowed. The look in her eyes was unfamiliar, but soon I would know its source. In some beautiful and mystical way the presence of spirit granted us permission to be still so the story could be told. She said that in the middle of the night, as her dreams unfolded, a peculiar event found its way to her. There, standing by her bedside, were her departed family members. They graced her room with hope and gathered to tell her stories of what lies ahead. My mother in all of our years together never spoke of such things, certainly not with the conviction I see in her now. Mom, ecstatically, announced them by name to me as if I had forgotten who they were and we laughed together. She spoke their names out loud in case they were still listening, she said. She told me, without hesitation unlike any other moment before, that when she dies all of them will gather around her. They will form a circle, hold hands, wake her up and tell her it's time. I noticed every part of her smiled as she recounted the story of this wonderful visit that she needed to experience. She proceeded to say that they will know when it's her time even before she does, and she will know when they're here because the same calmness that is in her soul now, will be there moments before she leaves and beyond her passing. Mom said that they will guide her into the warm glowing light of heaven. "It's what they do," she exclaimed with a deafening joy in her voice that made me smile on the outside, and made my insides cringe at the idea of losing my mother. When she shared her words with me, all of the fear that had engulfed her tranquility years before had disappeared as if it never existed. Upon her final breath, when life is no more, her brothers and sisters with whom she missed so dearly will surround her in a soothing and wonderful light.

However, there is one singular person, more than any other, she longed to see and be reunited with. For the last forty years she waited, one night after another, for some vision or message directly from mother to daughter. Many of her nights were filled with anticipation and anxiety of an outer-body visit from the woman who gave her birth, but none had ever come. In my quest over the years to offer her encouragement about how we live-on after death, it wasn't until this particular moment that solace had become her armor. Her eyes welled up with tears, our hands embraced and finally my mother knew what I had said for so long, that in the darkest moments of life, a light will shine, you will live on, we will always be together and when one breath ends, another begins.

She leaned even closer to me, arms wide open to receive me and said "I love you." These three beautiful words filled every part of my being, bringing me to a place of amazing comfort. I guess that's what unconditional love does. It opens the heart, expands the knowing and eases the mind. It truly gives you a chance to craft another memory. Each memory allows us to reflect and simply teaches us how to live the very life we want to live. No matter what you know, who you are or where you've been, life is a grand mystery with no details of what it will be or when it will change. Was my faith being tested or was this part of my soul's migration to something I needed?

Unbeknownst to me, this would be our final conversation together. A mother and son conjoined by life was soon to change. As her son, have I given her all that I could have in life? Have I been devoted and caring, as she was for me? Because what she gave me was life itself, more precious than any other gift and its value cannot be calculated or compromised, no matter what kind of life you've had. A mother who devotes her life to her child and gives that child the best possible life is what truly matters.

I drifted back to starlit summer skies as we sat beneath a blanket of stars. The blackened sky dazzled us for hours with a spectacular interstellar explosion of light. We sat upon the porch talking about everything and nothing for hours. Shooting stars would waltz across the sky, the sound of the tree frogs would sing their song to one another and the pine trees would perfume the air with their sweetness. These were perfect days together. She especially loved waiting for the rain to bombard the grass with nourishment. With my eyes closed, I can see us sitting there again, listening to the symphony of sound that the raindrops delivered, and I had another exquisite memory to cherish.

I began a conversation, in our last hour together, about the beautiful lights, referring to the night stars, we watched sitting on my porch. I think the stars all get bright when someone passes on, lighting the way to the next phase of our journey. I know that many gather to guide us and angels encourage us to move ahead. They show us that the love we started does not end when we die. My mother will be mothered again. Distance and time, pain and suffering and despair will not be adversary opponents anymore. In my head, I heard her say that when I sit on the porch one summer's night long after she's gone the wind will brush up against my heart reminding me of our treasured times together. When she falls asleep on a day not far in the future, her eyes will open in heaven and the stars that she gazed at here will guide her there.

Finally after all of my years of offering my mother the possibilities of eternal love, it now becomes her own private revelation.

Three

Time Is Now Measured By Minutes

O ne hour ago, the hospice nurse said that there may be another twenty-four hours left. Imagine the possibility of only twenty-four hours left of a life lived. I can barely comprehend those words.

After a long vigil of support and gentleness offered to my mother my body calls for rest. Rest is my friend and time is my enemy. With little choice, I find a nook of space in the back seat of my car parked in the nursing home's parking lot, and begin a time of solitude and prayer. But what do I really pray for? Do I pray for one more day with her because it's what I need or do I ask for God to be kind to my mom as she bids us farewell?

Do I ask for my mother's voice to be returned to me or do I pray that she be set free from her physical captivity? So many questions filtered through my mind, none answered! Fifty years of life and now I face the inevitable, the loss of the one person who has been there every single day since my arrival. I am on the forefront of having to face my greatest fear, life without my mother. What should I do right now? My body needs rest, my soul needs ease and my heart needs peace, all of which seem to be so far into the distance. My mother lays in her Earthly cocoon waiting to be reborn somewhere else and I am in my pain and agony in the here and now.

In my quest to understand the process of loss, I must open the doorway to self-tenderness and awaken a spark of self-compassion. We walk through a myriad of obstacles associated with grief often not knowing how deep the grief is penetrating our being. Sometimes it is easier to cast aside the pain versus walking into it directly. Grief exposes our vulnerabilities; it's not a weakness, it's part of our human condition. We love each other and the connection runs deep, causing every cell in our body to experience the throbbing pain of someone's death. Not even one's imagination prepares you for such things.

Grief starts at a nursing home with your elderly parent, in a hospital room with a terminally sick child, at home with your demented father whose Alzheimer's disease is in full throttle or an illness that has no cure.

Each of these circumstances begins our partnership with grief. As I contemplate the position I'm in, I realize I am still my mother's child and the idea of not hearing the cadence of her voice frightens me.

There's a book I read years ago sitting high upon a rock deep within the tapestry of trees. It reminds me of what my mother had said days ago. In the book the author comes to discover that her life will be born again. She doesn't know how, but knows it deep within herself. My mother had become the author of her life's story and she beholds a garment of new as she releases her physical body to spirit. I tried to hold within my concentration my mother's vision some days ago, but it doesn't seem to help my heart pain. I remember that her face was sprinkled with relief and the markings of tension that painted her face had disappeared. Shouldn't I be happy for her?

A knock on the car window shudders me to the bone. My long-lost slumber is halted by the deteriorating condition of my mother's health. She is closer to the threshold of her physical demise and nearer to the freedom she so desperately needed. As I rub the sleep from my eyes, I want only to think of myself. But somewhere my mother's voice has found its way to be heard inside of me. In a dream-like moment she tells me that I will be alright through all of this. Imagine, in my years of offering messages to those in need, my mother is now the messenger knowing exactly what spiritual memorandum I need.

My mother's wisdom cascaded through my mind and through my soul as I removed the jacket that covered my worn-down body during rest. A flash of light had glistened in my car and instantly brought me back to childhood memories that have been hidden beneath a sea of life. There's a little boy running up the driveway as he waves frantically to his mom on the second floor porch. She smiles, smokes a cigarette and is happy that her boy is home. Flickering lights continue in my daydream, like a spectacular fireworks display, one after another. Memories that had disappeared with age seem to find their way back to me. Just like a lightning bolt scurrying across the sky, so does one memory after another filling me with so much remembrance. There's a 12-year-old boy sitting at the dinner table happy to be home, to be loved and to be safe. Her gestures, smiles and love made me feel complete. Another memory flashes before me: a young man walking towards me in his cap and gown, and his mother emits pride that could fill a football field a thousand times over. Memories are specks of time— dewdrops of life—giving each a chance to remember that we existed together.

Another knock pounded my window, this time with more force than the last one, announcing that I must get to her bedside immediately. I find myself running back to her room hopeful that she is still with me. Tears flow from my face, knowing that this is my last day with her. I realized that I spent the last hour meandering through my memories of a life lived. I was walking the old paths of life, reminiscent of days together and remembering the love of the life I had before this very, very, dreadful day. I also recognized that my last hour alone was filled with my mother, daydreaming of the moments that made my years.

I'm back in her room and to my amazement she is still alive. Her body barely capable of its respirations, but it didn't matter; I still needed her to be here. I checked my watch to see how much time had passed and minutes turned into one hour. It's now 2:00 PM.

Four

Longing for More Time

T he sound of the harmonica plays softly, each breath creating a quietude that invaded my fears. Collectively the musical notes stretched across the nursing home unit and deep into the heart of the onlookers, all of whom who have come to her room with their walkers and wheelchairs simply to ask if she's okay. Sadly, there's no more time to buy, no more moments to steal and no more good-byes. Each second of her life has been accounted for, every step that she has taken was a tribute to her place in this world. Every decision she's made was hers and hers alone and there was absolutely nothing I could do to change the circumstances of what tomorrow would look like.

As I lay my head upon my mother's shoulder, I am back at her apartment two years before. She always wondered what purpose God had for her here, especially during the years of hardship. "Why am I here?" became her daily mantra, questioning why God hadn't "taken" her long ago. And, I, in my limited wisdom, told her that she had lives to touch, people to help and others to know, just like the rest of us. She half-smiled at me, cracked some joke and contemplated my words.

Isn't it true that each and every one of us has a purpose in life, no matter our age? Hidden deep within us is a compassionate need to serve others, to love without condition and to be part of the spiritual, global family. Whether you're serving humanity by feeding the hungry, loving a friend, nurturing the sick, bringing peace to the world or preparing stuffed peppers for your neighbors, your effort created from a place of devotion brings us back to our oneness, brings us back home. When comfort is offered, you cause a ripple effect of love that seems to be far-reaching than where you stand right now.

Days later Mom called with a sense of jubilation and celebration in her voice. She spoke of the dream that filled her slumber with delight regarding her place in this world. Her dream was filled with a majestic and nurturing voice announcing "there will be five special people you will help before you die." She didn't know who, when or where, but believed that her dream was a gift. The light that had diminished, in her eyes, was reignited again.

Seasons changed and she wondered if the people whom she shared her daily life with, at the high-rise apartment building, were the people she was destined to serve. She began to help some of her old folk friends along the way. As I remember the many stories; she offered bread pudding and stuffed peppers to those who didn't have food; she gave rides to those who didn't have a car or didn't have money to pay for a taxi. But most impressively, in her days of loneliness, she nurtured the lonely, sharing war stories of a life overloaded with more worries than joys. In the midst of serving others, she was astounded to be the recipient of kindness and charity.

For what she gave in those days was outweighed by what she received. And isn't that the greatest blessing of all!

Life has taught me that there's a reason for everything, even the challenging experiences of our lives. As I stand at the threshold of my mother's passing, her grace renews my faith in spirit. Every person that has ever stood with me on the road of my life has come, not only to receive something, but to teach me a life lesson. Maybe they chose the road they walk so that I can gain insight from their experiences. So, I can be better at being who I am. Like the old folk friends who needed a companion, my mother needed them just as much.

Mom would often say I just need one more person to help. She searched for days, months and years to fulfill her promise before her fateful day when the leaves say farewell to the trees. I noticed an ease, in a person who spent many of her latter days in fear, as she reacquainted with her inner peace. As I am remembering my mother's spiritual encounter some years back when the voice spoke of her mission to help others, could she have been number five?

I realized that I'd drifted deep within myself while my mother was trying to escape from her physical confinement. The bed that had held her, safe and sound, could no longer contain her. Her spirit was beginning to reach across the galaxies to some divine sanctuary far above the ground on which I stood.

Memories that have been my anchor are now camouflaged by pain as I'm reminded that our physical bodies cannot sustain life, no matter how much we pray. I'd offered my silent mediations and prayers days ago wishing that she'd communicate with her eyes but they are silent, too. A prayer is a step on the journey to faith, believing and knowing that your sacred thoughts, words and whispers are being heard. Your prayer reverberates through space directly into the heart of heaven. My prayer was for one more day with her, but God had other plans.

Seven minutes past two already, and the light within her is touching her destiny. The doorway to heaven opens a little bit more, a ray of hope brightens her way, and the fragments of illness and suffering are diminishing. The light of heaven gleams profoundly in my heart, causing me to be still. What can I say to her to ease her burden about leaving us or what can I offer her that will shed any residual fear about the journey that is in front of her now? I placed my voice near her ear, my hand upon her heart and the sound of my breath within reach. I whispered my gratitude knowing that my voice will be part of her forever. I shared my love as I have since conception and uttered that somewhere, very near, a light will shine, God will be standing there, your mother will be waiting and all who ever offered you love will invite you homeward.

Each second of time stretches across my consciousness. Every minute that passes by reminds me that time doesn't matter now. What matters is the love between us, the angels that surround us, the presence of holiness and godly energy when someone is dying and the kindness of so many that have come to wish her well on her new-found journey. She will, like all before and after her, be fitted with a vestment of golden light, a ceremonial robe or maybe her favorite blue dress; all are accepted attire in heaven.

It's twelve past the hour; soon she'll board angelic wings destined to soar beyond the agony of pain. A promise made long ago will be satisfied here when heavenly hands extend across the meadows of light and gently guide her to a healing sanctuary. A smile will illuminate her soul as she accepts the accolades for her courage and strength, and she will be born anew. Weightless, glowing and the essence of who she always was, will be the light that she shines forever. Ignited in this moment is her ascension between the vastness and the limitlessness, a place full of spiritual bounty. She stands, as we all will, at the threshold of a new day, a new time and a new beginning.

I lay my head down upon her arm, tears sweeping across my face and the sun begins to peak through the window. A bright light glides down from the wispy, fluffy clouds that dress the heavenly doorway into her room. Warmth begins to encapsulate me and she is closer to her physical demise. An unacquainted, but soothing voice echoes in my head "I will take care of her for you. You have done a good job." I raise my head to see who is speaking, but all who are present are crying. I look to my mother and the frustration that had become her armor is fading into the glowing aura that surrounds her. Can she see what I see? Can she feel the warmth of heaven's embrace? I reach back near her face and speak words to comfort her, but in fact, it is me who needs comfort, "Mom, heaven is right here. Heaven has always been here. Heaven is the tint of light in your great-granddaughter's eyes. It's the peace you feel when your body doesn't hurt. It's the special decorations made with love from your grandkids. It's the love that surrounds you now."

Wrinkles, markings of life, etchings of a journey she experienced and the road she traveled are fading into the serenity of the spiritual energy that embodies her. Prayers have been spoken aloud, songs have been song and unconditional love has been offered, but there is nothing to do now but wait. There is very little life in the woman I call Mom. She's no longer chasing her breath. It's now guiding her home.

Negotiations with God have stalled. It's now time to say good-bye to her. How do you really say good-bye to someone you love? I've tried so hard to remember the words and phrases that I truly believe in, words that I've shared with people searching for answers about life after death; like love is eternal—we matter to each other and, because we do, our love carries on. Death is not an ending, but a beginning towards the infinite—heaven is so beautiful—and they will always be with us. I have shared these words, but now I must cross the same bridge like all those I've counseled in my day. My faith, the prophetic words that I've chanted, and my knowledge of eternal love are stuck in the grief that overwhelm me because Mom is about to go home.

Five

The Gateway Opens

Drawn out moments come, one after another, announcing that she no longer breathes and I can barely breathe myself. The woman who has given me life has walked through the veil to appear on the other side of the continuum. The nurse places his stethoscope upon her chest and the evidence of life is no longer audible. With gentleness and care, he says "Your mother is gone."

Sixteen past the hour of two and the words "your mother is gone" crush me like a tornado passing by causing destruction to everything and everyone in its path and scorches my heart with unbearable discomfort. Pieces of my life had disappeared just as the nurse began to speak, memories that were mine were nowhere to be found and I wondered, for a brief moment, is this a dream?

Time is no longer pushing against me. It now retreats into nothingness. The hands of the clock cease from movement and the sounds of life evaporate into thin air, as if life had never existed before. I feel so wounded despite my work as a channel knowing how beautiful God's love is, how glorious heaven is and how love is not defined by the physical body, but by the bountiful love that is shared by two people.

As I try to think about how everything happens in divine time or there's a reason for everything in our lives or even words to ease my cracked heart that she no longer suffers, nothing provides respite for my broken self. I must be present in this moment recognizing that the earth we walked together belongs only to me now. I can feel the darkness of grief creeping into my soul. Mom has passed away, slipping quietly and peacefully from her worldly presence to a life of unparalleled love. And, what do I do right now?

Volcanic sorrow erupts and I am numb. No messages to channel from a mother's departure to her grieving son, no words to offer those in need and no spiritual intervention from a supreme holiness that she is safe. Only the physical experience of loss blankets my existence. I must learn to manage my seconds, nothing else is required of me.

Faces of family and friends crushed by the loss; my daughter falls to her knees in despair, my sister cries out with unrecognizable grief. All we can do is hold each other.

Loss is measured physically, not only emotionally. Your body will cry out in despair because every part of you is affected by death. The world in which we reside consists of physical possessions that we can touch, see, smell and hear. The sound of a mother's voice meant to alleviate fears is now muffled by death. A soothing hug a mother embraced her child with vanishes deep into the abyss. The smile of pride that lightened a face is never to be seen again. So, how do we resign ourselves that they are no longer physical?

In my quiet contemplation, as my tears saturate my face with disbelief that she has passed on, the sound of my mother's voice begins its destination back to my heart. Somewhere within me, around me, above me and beyond me is my mother. She is not separate from me, but part of me.

Our departed loved ones do depart from this physical reality. Their true essence, their smiles, their willingness to love us and the lessons they dispense will always be part of our evolution. My faith allows me to hold on to every particle of love that we enjoyed together allowing hope to build its foundation within me so that my future does not become desolate and barren.

I immediately feel the waves of grief, loss, sorrow and mourning, again, as I try to lift my head from her arm, but I cannot move. Everything is in slow motion, words sound garbled, my vision is fuzzy, as I cry out from the chasm of my pain, I begin a silent chant "Mom, follow the warm healing light to heaven. We will always be together. I love you." Like all who ever stood at this juncture she begins a voyage to a place far above the clouds and deep within the soul of the people she loved. And all we can do is pray for a sign, a message, a gift that she has crossed the artery of where souls meet spirit.

A gust of brightness filled my vision, nearly blinding me. The same holy light, witnessed many years ago when my own heavenly journey beckoned me home during a near-death experience, was here again.

Flaunting its sacredness, the light filled the room in which my mother lay dormant. A restless breath was no longer her shield, now she was everything she wanted to be. Peace etched every aspect of the room, despite the grief, the tears, the wailing of broken hearts and in spite of such spiritual terror, the brightness remained.

There is a soundless, innate promise that when one passes across the threshold of death, life is reinvigorated as you are greeted at the gateway. You are born and transported into your spiritual light, your memories are reawakened, and your heart-light begins its incarnation in heaven. It seems to me that everyone is offered the same eternal awakening, especially if you broaden the possibility that within you light exists. My mother, in all her years of praying for refuge, was now soul-to-soul with the heavenly authority that blessed her life with hope.

Memories resurrected from the darkness are coming back to life as the holy light encapsulates me. Thoughts, remembrances and life experiences parade in front of me like a Sunday afternoon matinee of your favorite old time movies. Breathing this holy brightness seems to bring me back to life and reconnects energy through my body again.

With my head perched upon her right arm, pictures of the old Christmas tree that decorated our apartment years ago remain like a still life photo. It's dazzled with stringy silver tinsel that suspended throughout the tree, most likely placed with great precision. The old nylon stockings filled with goodies hang attached to our bedposts waiting to be discovered. What joy her effort brought us. Despite her inability to provide us the most fancy of things, she knew what would bring us the most bliss. At this moment I'm discovering how precious those moments were and how precious those memories are. My mind had become vacant of them until I was reminded of their significance. Memories: they make you smile, laugh, and cry; but most importantly, they retell the story of life lived together.

My emotions are electrified beyond oblivion and another reflection of memories causes me to lose my breath. The old silo built over thirty years ago stands erect in the room of our favorite restaurant. Nothing planned, nothing scheduled, just the company of a mother and her son.

My eyes are drawn to a white light that penetrates my vision. I feel, instantly, illuminated inside. I look towards the doorway of the room that is filled with reminders of an old barn, and a cute little dog sits wagging its tail. I think to myself, "Oh, my God, they allow dogs in this restaurant?" I look again to my absolute amazement and discover running joyfully wagging her tail, surrounded in an awesome bright white light, fur fluffy and with a smiling face is my mother's long lost companion of some 30 years ago, an apparition appears and her beloved dog is here in my vision.

I immediately announce mom's dog's presence. Her eyes well up with tears, and she is barely composed.

"Mom, your little girl is sitting right here with you, gazing at you and wagging her tail like crazy. Your dog is filled with so much beautiful light because you loved her so and you had the courage to let her go. I am supposed to tell you that she'll greet you at the heavenly gateway when the time is right."

My mother begins to tell me the story of how she was going through her dog's photo album recently, crying uncontrollably of her loss and grief that she could no longer save her dog. She asked for forgiveness days before this encounter; none of this was known to me.

Many people doubt the existence of eternal love or the continuity of everlasting connections, Mom was one of those people. The idea of life after death, the hereafter or the heavenly resting place, became part of her consciousness on this day. These were moments of time woven together by a force greater than me. The conviction of a prayer whispered days ago within the security of one's thoughtfulness brings the power of a message, an answer that bridges grief to peace. Whatever mystery lies around the bend, messages have the power to begin a time of ease. My mother contained her despair and grief over the loss of her beloved dog, Tasha. As we drive home, she put her hand on her heart and said, "I feel better."

I'm startled back to reality, back to my mother's nursing home room, by the sounds of anguish that ricocheted from one heart to another. I look back at her, the twinge of pain is no more and an overwhelming sense of stillness enters my being. Is this peace I feel? Did her beloveds carry her home as they declared some days ago? Has she entered the promise land where souls meet God, where light is endless and love is undying?

Six

16 Minutes Have Gone By

Nine hundred and sixty seconds have gone by since her departure into the heart of heaven. Every second was palpable beyond belief. My eyes are swollen from gut wrenching sadness and the air I breathe is devoid of my mother's breath. But what can I do, she's gone. I'm deeply entrenched in negotiations with God, again, as I have been through the last forty eight hours, but now I pray for myself and those who suffer beside me. The attachment between mother and son, between our departed loved ones disappears at the time of their passing, or does it?

Emptiness and aloneness become your comrades as you establish a new way of living. Right now it's hard to fathom life without her. With each breath I inhaled, I tried to recapture every droplet of life we've shared together. I desperately wanted to go backwards to some familiar place where my mother's influence was still tangible, where her eyes were still twinkling with adoration for me and where her hug still held me. But that day is no more.

The loss of someone you love creates a litany of emotions, thoughts, questions, reactions, and everything in between. The person you were at the moment of their passing shifts. A boy becomes a man and a girl becomes a woman, no matter your age or the relationship you shared. When a mother passes away or a child dies or a grandmother leaves this world, the circle in which we exchanged life will forever be altered. Yet the idea of Mom being surrounded by angels strokes my soul with comfort.

Mom's deceased loved ones promised, during a nightly visit only four days ago, that when her eyes closed on her final day, they would encircle her, gently wake her up and carry her home. Believing in that promise fueled my mother's courageous determination to enter the next step of her life with grace and wonderment. The emptiness that had plagued her for years had left to blossom in a field of light. The divine light longs to aid heavenly travelers as they venture towards the entranceway to spiritual bliss. It waits until we have completed our purpose and our service here.

When you're grieving, memories of days past appear and reappear like flickering lights. Moments shared together seem to fuse with your thoughts and the reality of loss disappears, sometimes for a fleeting moment. In the days leading up to Mom's passing, she became my greatest teacher. The old ways of thinking dissipated into dust and no longer clouded her disposition. She led by example becoming the voice of spirit herself. She channeled grace, love and wisdom with her eyes, but more importantly with her touch. She had worn her joy like a gorgeous coat made of exquisite fabrics and in those final moments she cloaked all us with her love.

In my years of telling spiritual stories of loving continuity, I wondered if God, the angels and her departed family would uphold their promise. A promise is a sacred agreement generated between two people. The promise is realized every time a prayer is whispered or when a light shines upon a darkened road or even when one holds the hand of his dying mother. A promise blended with love opens every part of the soul allowing faith to grow. In my quest to discover the truth about spiritual communication and the everlasting connection that exists, everything I understood was now in a state of revelation.

Did they gather to create a circle of support so she wouldn't be afraid? Did they gently nudge her back to life as they promised? My head remained planted on Mom's arm. Waves of emotion from deep sorrow for my personal loss to joy for the peace she must feel right now flooded my mind. Often I've said to those in need that death is a doorway to a place of oneness that leaves you in awe. Heaven's beauty cannot be defined by a singular language. It's a place where hearts reunite, where love is uplifted and revered. Waiting to be awakened are memories warehoused within the soul, linking them to those who must stay behind and creating an unbreakable bond.

And there she stood on the threshold of heaven's gateway, embodied in a golden vibrant light, weightless and bursting with splendor. The juncture between life and death was crossed and the entanglement of living was no longer hers. With a radiant smile, she gazed deep within my soul, touching my heart with stillness and easing my suffering with strength. The angels mystically erased my grief for a brief moment of time and my fear of losing her had disappeared as her eyes spoke to mine. This moment was like a million sunbeams breaking through black and dark clouds blazing my brokenness with comfort.

After the harmonica ended its praise to Mom's passing, I sensed she was making her way back to me. I could see beyond the veil the semblance of a woman I loved so dearly. She seemed to walk with the same gait, smiled the same smile of adulation and murmured words that impacted every speck of my nucleus. Was I dreaming? Was I wishing for Mom to be here or was she corresponding through some method of celestial communication to fill my soul with ease?

With my head rooted in a pool of tears, a light began to shine through the darkened space within my heart. Though my eyes were blindfolded in grief, a mother's love for her child cannot be expunged from existence. Despite the demise of her physical body, her spirit was standing strong. She was no longer of the flesh, no longer restricted physically and bound by the love that began our quest together.

When our last breath ends here in our physical world, the sanctuary of divine love imparts the ability to breathe beyond the crossways. Heavenly inhabitants greet you before you leave, surround you with angelic wings as you bid farewell to those you love, whisper poetic inspirations expressing the continuity of love and guide you deep into the core of heaven's realm.

Mom's voice resonated within me. There was no movement, just her voice. It filtered through my doubts and fears causing me to realize that she was present. I felt such joy knowing that she was already delving into the brightest, most glorious, rays of light. This blessed ray of light realigns with your holiness as you receive its gift of unconditional love and leads you to the cusp of heaven's entrance. In this light you stretch beyond the possibilities into a place of knowing that you will carry on.

Mom spoke directly to me telling me that the angels gathered some hours before she left her nursing home bed. She said they remained encircled around us for the last sixteen minutes of her life comforting her so her transition to the after-life would be with as much ease as possible. The divinely ascendants had come to prepare her as she crossed from one dimension of the journey to another. They also comforted the broken hearted eyewitnesses with piercing reassurance that compassion is what guides the physical death of a loved one to the dwelling place beyond the sky. Mom was draped in serenity and we were bathed in the purity of everlasting love long after her final minutes transformed our world.

When our last breath is underway, the room becomes illuminated with the presence of our departed loved ones. They gather to tend to your reawakening into the heavenly sphere of light. The place of your passing becomes saturated with angels, guides and guardians whose purpose is to be your spiritual guide through the process of dying and death. When someone you love is dying, your mission is to comfort his/her body and soul, and the angel's agreement is to comfort his/her soul and spirit. Together we bridge an invisible chain of continuity that affords our loving attachments to be imprinted forever within the hearts of those left behind and those who live amongst the spiritual radiance. I held her hand in the last moment of her life and it is the light of God that carried Mom beyond the entranceway of heaven's door towards her spiritual paradise.

Every familiar voice that echoed in her life, her son, her daughter, her grandchildren, all her beloveds, was transmitted through a spiritual communique' engraving a permanent heart-to-heart, soul-to-soul connection never to be forgotten. She said the sounds of our voices telling stories from days past brought great peace to her as she was getting ready to greet her departed family and her beloved dog. The touch of hands against each other comforted her weariness. The gentle kisses from a son and daughter to a mother was a gift.

As you die, you receive a glimpse of the journey that lies beyond the breath of life. Mom said that every step you take someone guides you forward. As she spoke, a smile transformed my grief. She was beaming from heart to heaven with immeasurable fearlessness. Her smile exploded in a gazillion pieces of light that filled my darkness with hope. A smile generated from the depth of one's unconditional love radiates a shimmering glow of affection that is recognizable. Mom said, "I will remember you. I will never forget you guys."

She proceeded to say that in her darkest hours throughout life, it was her faith in God and her family that allowed her to live the best life she could live. When you die, you wake up in a place where gentle souls touch your heart, smile a thousand smiles and remind you that we are simply in the other living room waiting to be reunited. She was told, as I have told countless numbers of people during channeled messages, that when we are in thoughtful meditations about the ones we love, the doorway that adjoins the two rooms begins to open.

I knew Mom met all of those she longed for and I knew God would not fail my desperate prayer. Love does live on!

Seven

"Stuff" Doesn't Matter

O ne of the most amazing things about grief is how your memories of a life shared come without notice. Sometimes those memories bring tears and other times, laughter. As I was thinking about Mom and her contribution to my life, I found myself back at her apartment. She was about to teach me my greatest life lesson.

My mother entered her apartment for the last time; walker in tow, hands swollen, yet beautified with a radiant smile. I wore my sadness on my sleeve and barely could control my despair, but I remained strong as we decided what to do with her prized possessions. Her apartment, eight stories high, was her "castle in the sky." The thought that her home would no longer be a place of existence caused me great pain and I could only imagine what she was going through.

My emotions began to surface, tears climbing out of my heart soaking my face with wetness. I couldn't breathe. Her balcony was my only shelter as I tried to regain my composure and reclaim my serenity, and I did for nearly three minutes. From where I stand I could see the Blackstone River flowing towards an unknown destination. It moved with ease through the backdrop of trees, bridges and buildings to find some faraway place.

The river is strong and mighty and travels without interruption on the journey it must take. It doesn't know where it must travel or what it will touch, but knows that it must move forward. For some reason I feel comforted by the river. It reminds me that many people have stood where I stand today searching for strength from some universal source. Life moves, like the river, no matter what! I gaze at the diamond-like reflections that tumble across the top of the river. Mirages of light twirl across the greenery of the riverbank forming shapes and images that offered a moment of fantasy in a time of difficulty. This quiet meditation infused a knowing that no matter where you are, you are always part of the river. I will always be my mother's son even as she travels to some faraway place beyond the blue skies out of my sight.

I've been my mother's caregiver for so long, but how do I care for her now? In my years as a professional nurse, healer, and channeler of sacred messages, how could I muster up the courage to go back into her apartment and ask her what she wanted to do with all of her belongings? The releasing of one's things has such finality to it. All we can really do in moments like this is be truthful. Tell them that you hurt inside, honor your true emotions, cry on their shoulders, tell them you love them with every fiber in your being, and that life without them here will never be the same. With a gesture, smile and hugs, their strength will give you the courage to carry on.

Once the items are gone what's next? I know the imprint of life is etched on everything. An inscription embroidered into the soul will remain throughout eternity. The things she touched, I will touch. I am quite sure I will feel her again even when I hold her sweatshirt long after she's gone.

Everything we do, everything we touch and every experience we have together is embedded within the sacredness of our knowledge and remains in our hearts. Simply sitting with the memories of life will give you an opportunity to realign with them again. Often I said to people, "keep your heart opened." If we remain heart centered and opened then we have access, full access, to the beautiful life and memories we shared. Her favorite things will grace my room and for a brief moment the memories will ease the depth of sadness that grips me now.

I wondered what battle she was fighting at this very moment when neighbors would come in and offer sentiments of support. My mother, like all before her, was at a spiritual crossroads. This place has no questions, no answers, just a beginning. Her physical life will change into immobility and her spiritual life will ascend into freedom. Only when your departure from this place is nearby do you begin to understand the magnitude of the heavenly energy that exists in all dimensions. All we can do for those who face their immortality is shine love, embrace them and give their fears a voice so that their words don't get trapped inside.

Her tchotchke-filled apartment was decorated with handmade trinkets given by her grandchildren, items purchased at some Christmas bazaar or stuff found sitting at her door step. A collection of angel statues and family pictures seem to be her decorative theme as they filled nearly every wall of her three room apartment. With my broken, cracked voice and the anticipation of great sorrow for what must happen next, I asked her what she wanted to do with all of her "stuff." She paused, looked at her angels, stared at every sacred totem that she collected for a lifetime, touched every precious handmade artifact and held every framed picture, and said with teary eyes "I realized that this stuff doesn't matter. What matters to me is you. What matters to me is my daughter and my grandchildren." She proceeded to say that she will carry us with her wherever she goes and all of this is just stuff. "Stuff doesn't matter! What's really important," she said as she placed her hands on her heart and wiped her tears, "is the love that I feel right now. I have been so lucky to have you and your sister in my life."

The inanimate acquisitions are tiny reminders of a life traveled, but it is the love that binds us together forever. At that moment my mother released and relinquished the possessions of life as she cloaked us with unconditional maternal love.

As I share this story, I remember the love, too. Evoking the love and the sacred words that my mother offered her little boy on that day opened the doorway to a new way of thinking. When we remember the love, it allows a portal of light to shine through grief and darkness. It gives the memory a chance to blossom within us as energy, so that it becomes a tangible experience which nourishes us. It allows the essence of someone to remain with you long after they have left this place. Like the river, my mother is traveling to some faraway place, but as I stand at the river's edge I know she stood there, too.

Eight

And Now I Must Grieve

We parted ways some thirteen hours ago. Mom draped in a shroud of adoration and I covered in numbness. Red carnations bejeweled her hands, and like any good son, I simply walked her to the entranceway of her mystical spiritual journey. The sweet scent of her favorite fragrance perfumes the air I breathe and the night wind seems to call her once more. Somehow she presses against my heart reminding me of how much she loved me and that our lives were just beginning.

I can only imagine what she feels right now as she looks back at the faces of those who truly loved her. Her smile radiates within me and heaven, I bet, is a tad brighter because of her. On the path of our lives, our departed loved ones leave a glint of light showing us the way. And they will forever be ours.

There's such stillness in my room tonight. Sleep escapes me. I walk aimlessly across the carpeted floor hoping and praying for an ounce of thoughtless slumber, but this is not that time. In the distance beyond the window pane, drifting far from my grasp is a brilliant, omnipresent light. As I adjust my vision towards the darkened sky it slowly transitions to day. The twinkle of night has gone to sleep and I must face my first day without her.

Morning has broken through the dread of night. My body aches, my mind feels wrecked and my heart barely beats, but it is my tears that seem to hold me hostage. The sun is finding its way past the trees; birds are in flight and their shadows paint the grass with a carbon copy of their wings. However, this is unlike any other day and now I must grieve.

How does one really grieve the loss of the one person who has known you beyond conception? How does one find the strength to walk through the darkness of loss back into light? How do you master the ebb and flow of another life cycle? I have given deep thought to these questions for years. I, like all who have lost someone dear, will honor my faith knowing that love has the power to be immortal.

I keep the essence of my mother's spirit within my understanding since this is the only aspect of her that will never be stopped by death. As waves of grief bury me, I try so hard to recognize that love exists in every speck of time and space. All I need to do is keep my heart open to receive those magnificent sparks of love, and somehow I will find my way through my sorrow.

My spirit knows that Mom will live on, but the little boy who longs for his mother needs to be patient and self-nurturing as he readjusts to his new life. Anyone who has lost someone to death must face the next day with whatever their faith and strength tells them. My faith in God and my life as a spiritual healer, sharing sacred messages of hope and eternal love, offer me solace as I circumvent my grief to a place of respite. I've shared with many people that eternal love stretches beyond the possibility and deep into the reality of this moment. I must continue to witness this knowing every single day from this day forward, as you must do in your own lives.

Love is the only truth that lives within us. It is this love, shared between two people (between a mother and son, a daughter and father, a grandson and grandma), that expand our ability to walk towards healing after someone passes. In my attempt to work through my grief, I reacquaint myself with all of the love we shared together in our lives. And this offers me peace.

Minutes turned into hours and days into weeks before I would be blessed with a gift from heaven, a sign of eternal love. I often found myself driving deep into the woods of Connecticut, through forested roads filled with pine and naked maple trees, simply to find a place where I could cry. I would drive for hours and hours in the same neighborhoods longing to be seen and needing to be alone. I was sequestered within the confines of my vehicle. No one knew of my suffering.

A few people since Mom's passing said, "Thank God, you're a medium. It must not hurt as bad because you can still see her on the other side." And others voiced their opinions that my reaction of grief was surprising to them because of my faith in eternal love. Every human being, including those who believe in God and the world beyond this world, experiences grief. As part of the human condition, grief translates into pain that affects every aspect of your being. I wasn't afforded a golden ticket free from the sadness because of my faith or the work that I did. I needed to accept the humanness of loss and begin my journey towards peace. Although I understood the concept and realization of spiritual communication and divine messages, I was still my mother's son and I was feeling motherless and alone during my time of bereavement.

Neighbors waved, people smiled, joggers jogged and life is as it was for them. I imagine they've lost someone, too, but this is my day to mingle with sorrow. My hands tightly clutched against the steering wheel caused my knuckles to turn white. I am breathing, but somehow I don't remember how to breathe. Tears create a tsunami of wetness soaking my eyes with an inability to see the road on which I traveled. I stopped my vehicle and I cried and cried.

As I sat in my car, I slowly regained my awareness, I realized that the weather had drastically changed. Torrential rain saturated the ground causing a profusion of flooding across the street from where I parked my vehicle. Gray and dark clouds hovered above me. The trees were dripping with raindrops and hail pelted my vehicle causing a curious symphony of sound. I noticed that the brook was raging as it moved over the rocks, underneath the broken tree limbs and close to the street's edge. The river moved, determined to find its way. Oddly enough, the scenery that surrounded me expressed the depth of my reaction to the anguish I was feeling. There was an eerie similarity to what I was going through, emotionally. The rain had flooded the ground and my tears had flooded my soul.

The sound of the raindrops and hail became hypnotic, creating a musical masterpiece for reflection and contemplation. I stopped crying and began to pray. My prayer was to create an intention of love for myself, my sister, and all those left to walk onward without Mom's physical presence in our lives.

As I was sitting in the car, unable to drive ahead because the weather barricaded me on the dirt road on which I parked my vehicle, the mystery of spiritual dialogue was about to unfold. I had an epiphany. Somehow it became very evident to me that Mom's life path was exactly as it was supposed to be, including the last four days of her life, her rehab care, her subsequent hospice care and her passing. She was blessed in ways that other people were not blessed. She had children who cherished her, and grandchildren who enjoyed her sense of humor, family who truly loved her for who she was in our lives. In the last two months of her life, for the first time ever, she found herself worthy to be the recipient of every bit of love we had to offer. The essence of Mom's love was now complete in all of us because of the circle of life we experienced together. Hurt, old wounds, regrets and sorrows were now completely healed by love in all of us.

Immediately after your loved one passes, grief steals your solace causing pain and disharmony. It is the love that you shared with your departed loved one that remains the natural healer gently bringing us back to solace. Memories that were full of life fade into nothingness. It is love that never fails you. Love is imparted within the soul of each person and when that love is given solely for the purpose of loving then serenity finds its way back to you.

I remained in my car imagining a gold thread of light that mystically found its way to Mom's soul. Somehow through the mystery of life, living, loss and death, that same thread of gold light would find its way back to me.

Celestial music filled my car with enchantment, the weather remained unchanged, and tingling feelings overwhelmed my body. An avalanche of emotion continued to cascade through my minutes fueling my next hour with severe intensity. I could not move. I could no longer pray. All I could do was be silent.

Visions of a little ten year old boy dancing around his apartment singing songs grazed my thinking. Days of joyful celebrations filled my mind with wonderment. I began to find a smile tucked deep within the crevasse of my unhappiness. Our last Thanksgiving Day pierced my heart reminding me of how fortunate we were to have one more Thanksgiving with Mom. Despite one tear suspended from my eye, I remembered that day with great fondness and love. We laughed, and then, she laughed. When she cried, we cried. We all knew, deep inside, that this would be our final family gathering. As I was basking in my thoughts, my memories, all of them, good and challenging, reminded me that Mom did, in fact, live life.

Energy restored my spirit. My brokenness remained shattered, but somewhere inside the grief it changed into a light shining its brightness. The feeling of being loved surrounded me. It was like the feeling you get when someone you love holds you close, or when there's a spiritual presence blessing you. There, joyfully, enshrined in the holy golden light was my mother. A vision of maternal love embraced me. I bellowed with unbounded bliss, "Mom, I love you so much. I miss you. You are radiant! What are you doing here? You're supposed to be in heaven getting settled! Are you really here? I heard her slightly charged, snippy but humorous voice deep within myself say, "Can you see me? Then, where do you think I am?" I found myself laughing in the car as we gazed into each other's souls.

There's an imaginary bridge that crosses the threshold from life to death, from Earth to Heaven, from heart to heart. It's the bridge that carries us through our lives, guides us towards each other, inspires us, supports us when grief is our only expression, awakens our soul to the splendor of heaven and sends us a golden thread of eternal messages.

Nine

"Ask and You Shall Receive"

I've always believed that when we ask for something it will be there for us. A prayer or even a wish is always answered in the right moment of life. The real question is how do you see what is present in your life or the gifts of spiritual communication when grief and sorrow remain so overwhelming? Since I've started my journey of grief and loss, it requires a conscious daily prescription of self-love and acceptance that life has changed.

The tall pine trees that line my property are still green, rising high above the house, just as they've always been. The flowers that radiate fragrance and color still rise from the earth, summoned by the sun's light. The moon finds its way from the east to meet the stars every night, but life has definitely changed! Mom doesn't live in her birth place anymore. She has moved away from her earthly residence to her heavenly domain. She may be a bit further now than I would like or is she? Does the loss of someone allow us to feel their love differently (or less) than when they were here? When I am down in my grief or living in my peace, in both instances I feel the presence of my mother's unconditional love.

Love is what remains when someone passes on. When I breathe, she breathes with me. When I cry, she consoles me. When I laugh, she is in joy. She does not live in some distant or remote place far above my grasp. Mom is part of me, as are all of our departed loved ones. Because love is offered without the interference of pain, suffering or grief, it truly becomes unconditional. The true gift is that our loved ones remain a part of our existence. It's up to us to learn how they are communicating with us and to see the mystical, spiritual signs that influence our lives.

There is no doubt that every human being experiences grief when a loved one passes and there is no doubt that we cannot move through this kind of suffering without the support of others. Friends, family and sometimes strangers know exactly what to say and what not to say. I remember getting cards with beautiful sayings in them, as if someone knew the secret details of my suffering. I didn't know the sender on a personal level, but that gesture of care was greatly appreciated. Allowing those encounters and connections to support you during your healing can only help you see that peace is possible. Also, I found that respecting my private time, alone, in the quietness of the healing, offered pure moments of peace.

My long days and nights of sadness since Mom's passing had begun to ease. I was beginning to have days of absolute peace and what a pleasure that was from the darkness of bereavement. Thoughts and memories of Mom didn't fragment my soul as it did shortly after she passed away. Serenity opened my heart in remembering who and what we were to each other. I was finding my way back to life by holding the belief that love is never-ending.

I wasn't always sure why or even how, but one day felt better than another day. Each day offered a glimpse into what the journey from grief to peace was all about. Sometimes it lasted for hours and, to my surprise, even days. I found myself sitting on the porch or visiting a place that Mom loved. Somehow all of this supported my grief. I really began to understand how specific and individual grief is for the person who is suffering. What helps one person doesn't always help another person. I did what I needed to do to find my breath again.

Winter was back. Cold and frigid air surrounded me night after night. The snow somehow didn't fall much the winter after Mom's passing. I thought maybe Mom had something to do with that. The idea of that just made me feel better no matter how ridiculous it sounded.

I would sit for hours wrapped in a down comforter underneath a blanket of stars. The night air was so clean and fresh. I would sit in silent peaceful meditation; praying, contemplating and finding my way. The season of winter immediately after Mom's passing, would shine the brightest stars, more than anytime I could remember. I would gaze deep into the dark night sky hoping and praying for a shooting star, a message from above, a white feather floating down from the sky or some spiritual something to get me through the night, but no message came during my time of silent vigil.

Despite the lack of direct messages, it didn't halt my understanding that love is everlasting or diminish my faith in something greater than myself. I was a little boy learning how to communicate again. I was learning how to translate my life experiences into sacred messages. Every person has the same opportunity to seek the light from the darkest experiences of life. It takes time and care, nourishment and attention, but more importantly, it takes perseverance and understanding that you are connected to the eternal flame of heaven's light.

Life had changed and I, like all who stood on the road to bereavement, was trying to reclaim my life beyond the grief. Every day I could feel the grief nudging its way back in, so I just talked myself through it by saying "It's okay to be sad right now." I allowed the sadness to be present. I nourished the sadness by remembering how much she loved me. I shared my sadness with those willing to hear me cry and I spent many hours in quiet conversation with my faith. All of which helped me to secure my inner peace.

I wasn't peaceful that Mom was gone. I wasn't peaceful that I felt alone. I wasn't peaceful as I tried to redefine my life. I found my peace in knowing that Mom was no longer restrained by anything. Life didn't hold her back from what she needed to do. I often felt that her passing would finally give her a chance to be a beacon of love, no longer consumed by fears, physical pain or whatever brought her spirit down. She desperately, in life, wanted to serve and help others. Maybe in spirit she could truly accomplish this task.

My heart began to beat effortlessly. My breath was simple again. I was walking through my pain and suffering with my head held high. I did venture into each day honoring what I believed and somehow through it all, Mom would find her way to me.

When you're grieving, glimpses of spiritual messages come. A light flickers, a rose petal ends up on your doorstep or a song is played, all offering the possibility that there's more than what we know about life after death. Prayers were answered. Messages started to come.

Mom would appear, faintly, in a dream or two and I continued to feel lighter within.

Even in our deepest grief and suffering, messages of hope seem to find their way to us. "Ask and you shall receive," a well-known biblical quote was beginning to truly be part of my new found life. Beyond the brokenness of loss, a message awaits. A visit from a departed loved one infuses your dreams. A feeling that someone is watching over you brings ease. A spiritual sign like pennies from heaven, butterflies or some other mystical message finds its way to us. It then becomes our responsibility to carry on the relationship by acknowledging with gratitude that the message was received.

I will never forget the day I was driving to my office. Time had passed me by and I was feeling stronger. Grief comes. You cry and you move forward. You wait for messages. They come and you continue to move ahead towards your personal destination.

Despite my loss, I still needed to move forward with my mission and to preserve my own place in life. My daughter, my family, my friends and even my dogs needed me to be here, present in life with them. Mom expected me to carry on. Somewhere within me is an understanding that we must carry on to fulfill our personal destiny. In my years of listening to spirit, messages have always been about carrying on.

For some reason something triggered images of Mom's last days. I couldn't get it out of my head. I was consumed with unbearable grief, again. I kept thinking about how I would advise another in my situation, but I couldn't remember what I believed. It's funny, yesterday was a good day. The sun was shining.

The temperature was a bit warmer and the hope of a new time was in my heart.

Sadness emerged with a vengeance and I was overpowered by grief. I was knocked down again struggling to find the light within my shattered peace. One day you're fine and the next day you're not. Grief is like an amusement ride tossing you around without regard for your well-being. I turned on the radio to distract my mind. A medley of Mom's favorite songs by The Platters totally confiscated my peace even more.

Panicked, I cried out for help. One minute after another slowly moving time. Tears rolled down my face so much that I couldn't see, but I sat talking to her picture on my desk. Visions of her last three days floated in and out of my memories. I saw her in bed dying again, crying again, and staring at me with vacant eyes. I pleaded for support. I called out to God, to my angels and to Mom to stop this relentless torture of emotional pain.

In my broken, heart-wrenched, shattered self, I screamed as loud as I could, "Can someone help me, please?" Exactly thirty minutes later, after my dance with deep grief, my phone buzzed that a text message was coming through and it said "Roland, I am here for you if you need me."

Ten

A Spiritual Revelation

Hundreds of minutes have passed by since that fateful day when my desperate plea for support was heard. Imagine a message sent from a dear cousin to me at the exact moment of need. I was drenched in sorrow, barely breathing and lost. The message offered me an opportunity to step through my grief, surrender my pain and trust that I was being guided. It's my belief, along with millions of others, that with love all things are possible. Even a serendipitous moment like this one cannot be explained away or defined by circumstance. It was a gift. I felt alive, again. I remembered love, again.

Was that a spiritual intervention? Was it the handiwork of God? Was it the love of a mother for her son? Or was it just something that happened? Whatever that moment was, it became an invaluable aspect of my journey from grief to ease. Does it really matter how the message comes to us, as long the message comes? When a message comes from a place of love to support someone in need, then the presence of something divine must've been part of that moment. For me, that message lifted my heavy heart, dissolved my sadness and expanded my understanding that love is truly a gift.

Since Mom's passing, time has been measured by the small hand of a clock. Sometimes you see seconds passing by and other times Mondays turn into Saturdays in the blink of an eye. Half the time I didn't notice the days in between. I just wanted to be in the state of peace. When you befriend grief, you are required to do nothing but heal the grief. You are forced to live your new normal life after the loss of a loved one or the other choice is to become secluded in your suffering. I chose to live my, maybe new, maybe normal life, but without the sound of my mother's voice, the touch of her hand or the approval of her smile.

I became very conscious of time, more than any other period in my life, except for the anticipation of the birth of my child. There is a great awareness when a baby is making its way to you. You become suspended by time, waiting, wondering and hoping for a vision of the little person who will change the world in which you reside. Your normal life is now doused with new normal energy. When someone passes on, you wait, wonder and hope for some vision of the person you love to gently guide you through the numbness of grief. Your life is no longer the same. You venture forward knowing that your normal is now shrouded with a new energy of living a different life. We all are here to live, learn, grow and to love through all of our experiences, including the birth and the death of loved ones.

As a new dad, some twenty-one years ago, was I able to fulfill the needs of my brand new little baby girl? Was I able to go beyond myself to live consciously with her? As I stepped on my journey I became alive because I trusted that together we would just love each other. Life is about love. Death carries that love, mysteriously though it may be, through the ethers, into the stratosphere, beyond the boundaries and back into the hearts of those left behind. Love hovers above, stretches beyond and sits inside us, embedded permanently as a sacred totem of a spiritual union between two people who experienced love.

Interestingly enough, the death of my mother caused me to see love even deeper than I had only months before. I was beginning to understand the thousands of people who made their way to me, sometimes feverishly or desperately. All in search of the loving continuity shared with those that had departed. All I wanted to do was hold them within my embrace, console their pain and tell them I understand. I saw them differently, because I was one of them now. I was not just one who believed in the after-life, but I was, like them, trying to live with the knowledge that someone you love is not physically here.

I wanted to shout out to the people of the world to take the time to fully invest in each other. Time, they say, is short. After Mom's passing, the idea of expressing my gratitude to those I loved became a part of my spiritual practice. I wanted to bridge the gap between today and tomorrow. I wanted to encourage others to love fully, completely devoted to those with whom you share your life. The idea that love celebrated in life remains a part of us forever was as old as the hills. If we love today, that love becomes part of the universal heartbeat never to be forgotten and never to be left behind. This love cannot be tainted by grief. It can only rise from the ashes, stronger than ever.

Somehow, I'm reliving my memories again. I find myself drifting back to some place, somewhere back in time. Maybe I'm dreaming. Maybe I'm having a vision. I see Mom in a light. Every part of me smiles. Oh, too bad, I am dreaming. She is healthy, strong and willing to live her spiritual life now. She smiles, radiates a glowing light and reaches for my hand. She seems to be surrounded by so many that have nurtured her spirit. Her face is without the pain of life. Light emanated from every part of her soul. I hear her talking to me, it feels like I'm floating. I hear her call my name but her mouth doesn't move. I just know she's with me because her voice echoes in my heart.

Nearly sixteen weeks to the day, Mom reappears again. This time I was awake, preparing for an event in New York. I heard my mother's voice again when I was in the shower. I yelled, "Mom, don't come in I'm not dressed." I realized how funny that was after I grabbed the towel, shut the light and slammed the door. Mom was gone, not of this world anymore. A bit of sadness was palpable for a moment or two remembering that Mom had left her earthly existence to claim her spiritual life.

As I was in prayer Mom reached out to me and said, "Roland, I have to come back to serve." In my mind I thought of an answer and knew somehow she could hear my voice, too. With my thoughts, I projected the words "you live in heaven now and you must stay there since this is your new place." I felt her persistence and determination in telling me that she must serve. And, I heard this over and over again. Finally, I left to go to present spiritual messages to a waiting audience of fifty people. I was hopeful that they would feel reignited in love again as I was from my mother's visit.

It's around 11:30 PM, the night was long, and the presentation of spiritual messages was filled with tears of joy, sadness and everything in between. I was exhausted, not only because I spent hours offering loving support to those in need, but because I too, needed support for the grief that sat within my heart.

I made my way back to my room. The bed was covered with an antique quilt decorated with pink flowers. It was soft and inviting for a night of rest and recovery from my days of working through grief and assisting others through their pain. The pillow was as soft as a cloud and I instantly fell asleep.

There standing, yearning to be seen, was my mother. I found myself witnessing her golden hue of light, just as it was shortly after she died. She smiled. I smiled back at her. I drifted back and forth, from peace to joy, as she presented her words to me. I heard her words again, "I want to come back to serve you and your sister."

My dream continued. I had been traveling for days anxious to get home. As I entered my house, the dogs jumped for joy at seeing me. Mable cried out with a piercing yelp that I was finally home. What a reception of love they offered me. I peeked into the living room and Mom was sitting in her favorite chair. I said, "Mom what are you doing here? You're supposed to be in heaven." "I'm here to serve you because you've been such a good son. I needed more time to mother you and your sister." She said this with such tenderness that I started to cry. I proceeded to say "How did you get here?" She said, "What do you think...UPS?" And, we laughed. Mom held me tightly in my dreams that night.

I woke up the next morning just wet from crying. Mom mothered me in my dreams! I believed that Mom was somehow reaching out for me to tell me a story of her new-found journey in heaven. It was my mission to awaken my consciousness of her and all of the sacred spiritual messages that were mine. Messages come to inspire hope and to fuel our loss with healing. The series of events on that day were life-changing, and what was to follow, took my breath away and returned it renewed.

Two days later, on Thursday, after my extraordinary maternal visit, I called my sister to share my dream. I said, "Guess what happened to me two nights ago?" With great excitement, my sister said, "Wait a minute. I have to tell you something. Mom visited me last night and she told me that she wanted to come back to serve." I cried and cried and cried. Then I proceeded to tell my sister my dream, and she cried. Mom hadn't forgotten that we were her children. She remembers us, her journey and the love we joyfully bestowed on her. I realized that in life it wasn't always easy, but now there is absolute peace for my mother, and now for sister and me. I guess everything is possible.

I'm back somewhere within my memories again. Mom found her way to me many times. For some reason, it's September 2011. I see myself sitting in mom's hospital room. The room is filled with tubes, IV equipment, and medical gadgets just in case she needed something. An intravenous bag, half full, was attached to a tube that leads to Mom's arm to prevent dehydration. The sound of a respirator for the patient in the next room created a rhythmic chant of sorts. Mom's oxygen tube was connected, but hanging out of one nostril. We laughed. She was no longer bothered by such things. Despite the severity of her condition and dire need for medical care, she was about to change before my very eyes.

She stared peacefully at me, gazing beyond me and speaking to angels. She was gentle and her heart was deeply rooted in mine. Mere words cannot describe the journey she took me on as our eyes met in the hospital room. The promise of tomorrow was within her grasp and the ease of life was beginning to be tangible for her. She spoke nothing of the world she would leave behind, only the world that waits beyond the threshold of life.

Mom wanted to speak of forgiveness. She said she was sorry to my sister and me for the challenges of life. She wanted to release the burdens of regret and despair. She said she was searching for peace and praying for help to let go of, what she called, troubling times in her life. We talked about letting go of the old stuff. That the old stuff didn't help anymore or matter anymore, so why carry it around your neck like a noose. Say you're sorry to someone you need to and allow an apology to come to you, as well. It wasn't necessary to be in a negative inner space, not now, not ever. Every one of us makes choices based on what we know, feel, see, hear or discover. These choices become the road map of our life's journey. Choices were made, life was lived and now, you can let it all go.

She wanted to find forgiveness for those who hurt and abandoned her during her time of need and throughout her life. We spoke in length of how necessary it was to stand at heaven's gateway cloaked in a light, purely made of spiritual blessings, not of regrets. It was clear to me in the years of my work that to cross into heaven's glory you must relinquish the parts that feel broken and you must visit all the parts of life that were not loved. Releasing these things before we go lightens the load as we enter the light after death.

I told her that forgiveness was a gift you give yourself. To free oneself from the burden of all of that heavy energy is part of self-love and self-care. She asked if she was a good mother and did I forgive her for all of the challenges of life. She began to list them, as if she had been keeping an internal document of the deeds she did in her life. I looked at her and held her. I told her that "without you, Mom, I would not exist. Without your contribution to my humanity, I would be nothing. I forgave you long ago. I forgive you now. I will never hold you hostage for any of the imperfections of my life. You were the best mother that you could be, just as I am the best son that I can be. When you give what you can, in a loving manner, then you have received everything." A smile arose from her grief. My mother became a mother to my soul on this day. I made an innate promise to love. You either believe in love or you don't. I said, "Mom, there is no gray area here and I know you love me."

Life is mysterious. We never know where the path of life will lead us, but we know it will take us somewhere. If we allow ourselves to trust the inner voice that guides us, our faithfulness and the belief that love is extraordinary, then we will be lead through the peaks and valleys of our life experiences, including the loss of a person so beloved by so many.

Eleven

Lessons of a Life Lived and Loved

I found myself driving across a familiar roadway, barely keeping to the required speed limit. The road I traveled crossed a beautiful body of water that appeared limitless to the naked eye. To my left the reservoir meets the sky offering shining rays of brilliant and vibrant light that illuminated the edge of the reservoir. Light tumbled across the water creating a reflection of delight for my viewing pleasure. The clearest sky reached across the infinite universe reminding me that there is no end. Mystically the blue and clouded sky provided a mirage of images that dazzled the top of the water. To my right magnificent grand pine trees stand taller than any other I've ever seen which line the horizon, a family of ducks gathers to commune for a moment or two and the sun brightens nature's splendor. The presence of peace has finally found its way to me.

I've spent many days taking inventory of the lessons I've learned while courting grief. It's one of those relationships you really don't want in life, but it's there and it needs your attention. I parked my car adjacent to the fenced area allowing myself to view the water's edge a little longer. Humongous rocks appeared as if they were placed to barricade the water's edge from unwanted disturbers of its natural beauty. I sat quietly, appreciating the landscape. With my sun roof opened I became the beneficiary of the sun's light and warmth. I prayed, thanked God, and sat with my arms extended through the opened space in my roof, just to catch a breeze. I could feel the sun's warmth as it touched my hands. For some reason that feeling brought me back to the nursing home, many hours before Mom died.

I was in awe of the beauty that surrounded me and equally of the lessons my mother taught in her silent final hours of life. My mother found a way, in those days and hours, to teach me lessons that would forever remain engraved upon my soul. In her battle to die, she taught me how to live. Isn't that what death teaches us? It teaches us how to live our lives, fully engaged with each other. It teaches us how to be one with each other, and despite the vastness of the human race, somehow death tells us it's a very small world. We all experience grief and we all cry when someone passes on. It's part of the human condition.

Grief has taught me how to see, not only with eyes, but with my heart. When my mother's voice was silent, I decided to be silent, too. I held her close, covered her with warmth, as the sun did for me and allowed my heart to speak on my behalf. I found that Mom was more peaceful as she found her sacred dwelling place. She entered her vortex of everlasting and eternal love.

I see with a much clearer vision the meaning of life. We are destined to live loving each other dressed with compassion and kindness. When moments come that are not aligned with those things that are holy, and they will, we must continue to search through the valley of difficulty and walk directly up the mountain to where we belong. At the top of the mountain is where the sun shines the brightest. There will always be roadblocks and detours. These are gifts, too. I know that in my darkest moments, grief peaks through, a tear is shed, and I learn even more about whom I am and how I can better serve those around me.

Everything in life teaches us a lesson. With those teachings enforced we become the captain of our life path, co-creating with spirit a wonderful existence. I've learned that healing the past gives breath to the present and expands the possibilities for our future life. As my mother needed to be forgiven, I, too, needed forgiveness. Forgiveness is a gift that allows us to walk without the weight of regret, mistakes, despair or hurt. It surrounds us with a checkered flag of success that we have made it through a time of difficulty. In my years, I've rediscovered that loving is the key to true happiness. Fear is something that fuels negative energy. Love is the great healer that exists in all of us. The minute we release the old hurts, disappointments and discouragement, the light is restored and life is ours again.

I am a father, a friend, a companion, a confidante, an ex-husband, a nurse, a spiritual channeler, and I am my mother's son. I discovered in the last sixty-seven days of my mother's life, that I was enough. As I walked into my time of bereavement, this lesson surprised me the most. I give as much as I can, and gave Mom as much as I could. I gave to my mother, as she did me, every ounce of herself that she could. Her life before me by far was complicated, chaotic at times and challenging at best, but she, too, was enough. This discovery I made after she passed away. Life has many conditions, and sometimes love has conditions, too. I understood my mother. She made our lives better than the life she left. The next generation will have it better than what we had and they too, will remember, with appreciation, the struggles of their families.

I realized that if you give of yourself with every part of your heart and soul, lovingly and compassionately, then you've served someone very well. In life we are given the opportunity to serve, assist, help and nurture each other, and we should, that's what being human is all about. "It is in giving that we receive," words that have been spoken for more than two thousand years, have the power to transform doubt into belief. Mom was free. I could feel that inside my heart. The love and forgiveness gave her a chance to stretch through the veil of death directly into the essence of her new normal life.

A person that gives with the intention of giving has a chance to receive more than they've ever given. Mom and I made a promise to be there for each other through the good and the bad. She taught my sister and I how to be a family. Love is the thread that keeps the garment together. In my dreams, in the quiet whisper of my silence, I hear her say "I will always love you." The wind blows, but you can't see it. The grass grows greener, but you don't know how. A baby blesses you long before they arrive, and you wonder how that is possible.

I maneuvered through another period of grief. I made it because my friend called just in the nick of time. She said "I was feeling like you needed to talk, do you?" Again, someone out there made this moment possible, so I could get the support I needed to expunge the grief from my physical body, so I cried. Just like the old folks in the building that my mother checked on daily, she answered their prayers, in the right moment of time, too. Every life is worth celebrating. Everyone has a spark of divinity within them. Our job, as collaborators of life, is to help one person see the light within himself.

Our memories are like sea shells waiting to be discovered. I stood with my feet planted on the shoreline of the English coast some years back.

The edge of the water summoned me, so I stood as close I could without getting wet. In front of me, was the ocean in all its mighty finding its way to the shore. Its soothing sound and brilliant blue colors were mesmerizing. Behind me stood a cliff reaching out to the sky standing hundreds of feet tall and all I could do was admire its breathtaking beauty.

There beneath my feet were tiny gems which lined the beautiful sea shore for miles upon miles. I stood alone listening from my heart. Everything is possible when you listen from your heart. The mind is complicated. It distracts your emotions and causes you to question what you're feeling or experiencing. The heart is the vessel of pure enlightenment. I was thousands of miles away from home, but this one stone, caused my breath to stop and my heart to open even more. It was as if an angel had placed it right at my feet. There, showcasing its beautiful aura, in a field of millions of gems, was a heart-shaped rock. I smiled and heard "it's for your mother."

It was my final day in Mom's apartment. It was hard to believe that she passed before we could get this all in order. My emotions were rampant and I was barely contained. My grief wailed from somewhere deep inside of me. I was so sad that her physical life and all that it held was gone. The apartment was bare of anyone's existence. The vacuum, which could barely suck up dirt, was following the same carpeted path that Mom had walked for over ten years. Pictures were gone. Nothing of her life existed here anymore. I was broken, so broken. I heard look up, so I did. There traced on the white walls was an outline of a heart and standing just at my feet was a stone-shaped heart. Everything I believe in about signs and messages was fulfilled, quietly, in the emptiness of my mother's bedroom.

Twelve

When One Breath Ends, Another Begins

S even months have slipped away since Mom's final day. I never wavered, not once, in my spiritual belief that there's a God, angels, or that our departed loved ones remain on the continuum of the loving voyage that we started together here in life. I'm sure she's just a bit further, destined to enjoy her heavenly experience. Time has come and gone, memories lost were found, and I am no longer the same as I was before that mid-November day.

My mother's greatest joy was her family. She wanted me to survive beyond her death, as all mothers would for their children, and live my life to the absolute fullest.

She often would say during the last two months of her life, "Will you be okay, when I'm gone?" How was I supposed to answer that question? I never lost my mother before. I sat with those words as we held hands four days before she died. I told her that I would miss her terribly and I was afraid to let her go, but I knew somehow that I'd be okay. She wrapped her arms around me, stared so lovingly in my eyes, stroked my right hand and said "I will always be with you." She took her hand and pointed to her heart. I cried silently. She took her little boy in her arms, again, and comforted him, knowing that our years have only hours left.

Friends who have lost someone to death offered words of advice. I didn't understand them until long after Mom passed away. The severity of what loss really feels like can barely be described. The faces of the many people, who have attended my events, waited for a sacred message that love lived on seem to help my grief now and then. My understanding about eternal love did not prepare me for the depth of my grief. It was my assignment to step into my loss, surrender to my grief and begin a process of bereavement. It's what I had to do.

Jack Hawley's book, *The Bhagavad Gita: A Walk for Westerners*, says, "When the matter part of this union falls in death, the spirit part remains standing." I will remember Mom's passing with reverence for her bravery and courage, but what I will carry with me through eternity is her essence, her true spirit. This part of us never dies.

The Tibetan Book of the Dead says "that one day there will be a great celebration when someone passes because they are finally free from the physical limitations." I will celebrate Mom, her life, her passing and her contribution to my life, until we meet again. She had the courage to leave behind what she treasured the most, so that we could live. Mom finally resides in the holiest place of all, in the memories and hearts of those left here to live life. It is our duty to carry on with as much happiness and joy as we can. This is what our loved ones expect of us. It is what's needed.

Shortly after Mom passed, I waited with anxiety and trepidation, as most grief-bound people do, about her walk into the light. I wanted to know it all immediately. But, in time, all that we need to know will be ours to bathe in. A morsel of love will shine on the dimmest day, brightening the sorrow with the heavenly light of peace, and then, and only then, will we know the truth. The deep truth is that their love for us will be the guiding force maneuvering through our life experiences.

My faith has taught me that in our last hours of life and in the first moments of death, angels and loved ones come to guide us toward the universal loving splendor that adorns heaven. Simply stated they guide us "to the pearly gates." I knew that she would, joyfully, see this as an adventure once her fear was no longer present and the realization that she, too, can see, feel and experience the ones she loved so dearly. Mom's fears left the moment her breath began in heaven. All of us who walk amidst compassion, kindness and lovingness find the heavenly domain beyond the final physical moments of life, and somehow see life anew.

As she lay silent in bed, we made it our mission to surround Mom with so much love and tenderness, then miraculously through the power of that unconditional love, her fears disappeared like they had been absent her whole life, as if she didn't recognize it anymore. Peace was everything she longed for and love truly erased the stain of fear.

My faith in God, knowing that he will love my mother, is a gift to me. I often think about God as a father. Wouldn't your father want you to be cared for in your darkest day, especially as you grieve a loss? Wouldn't a father do everything he could to erase your weariness, so that you could feel ease inside? And, wouldn't he tell you that she is safe in heaven? I believe that sacred messages are a gift from God, helping us to cope with loss of a loved one.

When a loved one passes, our mind, heart and soul become impatient in waiting for messages. I've missed her every day, and wondered how I could possibly emerge from such a broken place, but I did. I found parts of my life that didn't exist after Mom passed away.

Adult children who become caregivers of their ailing parents begin a process of redefining who they are without their loved one physically present in their lives.

I was one of those people who spent much time reclaiming my own life after Mom passed.

Occasionally grief peeks its weary head, but in time grief gets quieter as you embark towards acceptance. Soon the peace and knowledge of everlasting love will stand in the foreground as a constant reminder that you have weathered the storm of sorrow.

In our humanness, we cry when someone passes away. It's what our body does to expel the grief. You have every right to cry, to feel the pain of loss and then to release the pain. Once the pain begins to release, you must always make room within yourself for love. Fear, grief, pain is on one side of the spectrum. Love, joy, freedom is on the other. In time, and in healing, you will see your way back to love, back to peace.

I found myself crying in front of strangers who came to hear messages from their loved ones. Every time I spoke to a son who lost his mother, I was reminded that Mom had died. I relived my loss at every single event that I held from the moment Mom died to this very second. I also found peace knowing that my grief, despite my ability to channel loving messages, was normal.

My belief in otherworldly beings, such as guardian angels, told me that I would not succumb to the pain of my grief. Some people were surprised by my reaction to grief because I believe, so deeply, in life after death and others said, "If you can cry, then I can cry, too." Grief is a journey, unexplainable in how you will react, but you will react. It's an experience that cannot be waged without the presence of faith or support.

As I sat at my desk, contemplating the final chapter of my story and writing the last words of this extraordinary journey "I was here again" an unbelievable sign found its way to me. As I looked out the window, beyond the birch tree, towards the sun, a mother deer and her fawn, Mom's favorite animal, were just a few hundred feet from me grazing on the green grass and wildflowers that were on my property. I wept. Another moment of gratitude emerged. I rediscovered, since beginning this literary and emotional journey on Mom's birthday some five and half months ago, how precious life is and that we have a responsibility to love each other in the best possible way. As the mother and her fawn grazed on the palate of soft green grass, I felt such peace knowing that somehow through the mystery of living and dying and of life shared Mom is still with me.

After Mom passed, her favorite animal would find its way to me. Not once, but literally, hundreds of times. In the strangest places, deer would gather on the streets I traveled for a nightly reunion of sorts. Families of them seem to be waiting for me to arrive somewhere, and they stayed long enough for me to greet them. They stopped and stared at me for minutes upon minutes, more than just being stunned by bright lights. They seem to find their way to me when my grief was at its peak.

In one night, on one of my frequently traveled roads, there were seven of them. A deer standing tall with such grandeur, head raised and dark brown eyes stared at me for what felt like hours. Somehow he beckoned me to see him and to see his kin, and I did. As I looked back through my window, with my story complete, mother and fawn, gently walked into the wilderness, bound by an inseparable, invisible link called love.

The cycle of life continues. When one breath ends, another begins for all of us. I was beginning to surface from the depth of my broken heart. Mom was undoubtedly, breathing the air of heaven's bounty and the sun was shining bright again!

I could see the colors of the flowers, as if my vision was clear now. The magnificent dark pink lilies have found life, too. From a bulb, they sprouted into this gorgeous, statuesque six foot blossom. The wind often hovered so I can breathe in the fragrant beauty of the lilies. The primrose with their beautiful yellow petals, have come and gone, but they too will be back. And, the roses still perfume the air I breathe with their glorious aroma of sweet tomorrows.

My days of grieving are not complete, but the weight of despair has lifted. I smelled the spring air and felt the summer breezes once again. I sat upon my porch gazing towards the daylight and it delighted me with its beauty. The sunlight danced upon my heart and the clouds mesmerized my soul. I was finally in a state of stillness. I sat until night waiting for the fireflies to create a light show and for one breeze to capture my consciousness.

With my eyes closed, Mom stood aligned with me as she always has, heart to heart and soul to soul. A smile decorated my heart and I was here again.

Thirteen

After Words

T he one thing I know is grief never leaves you alone. It hovers above you and barely lets you sleep. It sneaks up behind you simply to remind you that your life has changed. It makes you cry at restaurants and doesn't allow you to listen to the old songs without shedding a tear or two. It infiltrates your time with heartache and sadness until you find your way through the pain.

So, how do we live through loss and grief, sadness and despair when someone we love passes away? How do we remember the memories without those memories causing us pain? And, how do we find our breath again?

The journey of grief is part of our human evolution. After many months of great personal sadness that unalterable fact has become clearer. Death is not an ending of love, but a relationship alteration between those left here and those walking heaven's pathways. Like everyone else, I had to learn how to take the knowing and make it reality again. I stumbled through my own grief, like a toddler learning to walk.

The journey of accepting the power of true and unconditional love is within us all and will be sustained even after the loss of a loved one. During the months after my mother's passing, I didn't always understand the how or the why, or where it would lead me, but I knew that I'd be shown the way through the darkness of grief back into brightness of hope. Grief does not discriminate against you or care who you are or what you know. It is what it is. Grief is an experience that every human being, who is bound by love, must go through.

It is our responsibility to forge ahead continuing life on earth. My knowledge of spiritual intervention and the heavenly connections offered me peace and solace during my days of deep sorrow. Knowing that Mom is now cloaked by the heaven's light gives me hope every time I am reminded that she is not here as she was before that fateful mid-November Day. Mom reigns high above the clouds and sits quietly, tucked within my memories, deep within my heart. She is part of every single moment of my new life; as she was from the moment I was conceived. This knowledge offers me freedom to live my life. We will always be together.

The essence of my mother, her love, her laughter and her true spirit, as with all of our departed loved ones, will never fade away from existence. Mom will remain a part of me until our eyes meet again.

A mother and her son, a daughter and her grandpa, a dad and his daughter are all bound by an invisible energy called love. Love makes us who we are and it is love that holds us together, even beyond death. We are not defined by death, but by how we love.

As unique as our fingerprints are, so too is our journey through grief. Trying to find a way through loss requires a steadfast and conscious kindness that only you can bestow upon yourself. In my days of working through my tears, month after month, it was evident that we each navigate our grief, sorrow and pain differently. What works for one individual may not nurture the next. The death of my mother showed me that my grief and tears are not different from the impact of personal loss on another human being. But how you heal through the loss reveals the next chapter of your life.

Why not choose to heal, to breathe, to find peace, to reawaken the life-force within and to honor the loving memories that cascaded through your awareness. I found it equally important to honor my sadness, my heartache, my grief and my loss. In doing so, the soul has a chance to find its wings again. Beyond the pain, fears and sorrow, lies a rainbow dancing across the sky waiting to be seen.

What is required is that you stay as strong as you possibly can. And, if you can't, it's really okay. When tiredness and exhaustion are upon you, take whatever steps you need to ease your brokenness. Stay in bed. Rest your mind. Sleep a little longer and allow yourself the opportunity to unveil the hidden light that appeared to disappear the day your loved one left this world.

Whatever it personally takes to work through your pain, do it. Don't hold back the tears; cry until the emotion is gone. Cry, and cry, and cry until someday your tears are replaced with a smile of adoration for the one you love and miss. Spend some time alone with the universe; I use to sit beneath the night sky communicating with the stars. It's important to give yourself the right amount of time to work through the different stages of grief and loss. And, it is as important to allow your true emotions to surface. Don't let them get trapped within the abyss of your grief.

It's true that sometimes you feel so alone and other times you feel lost. The way to heal is to acknowledge that these feelings exist. Sit quietly, breathe through your pain, and allow yourself time to heal the wounds of sadness. Sometimes a soothing voice helps, or gentle music creates an opportunity to sit quietly. Allow your emotions to have a voice, so that your light can be restored. Remembering the love you shared always allows another layer of healing to occur.

I found myself driving by Mom's old apartment, now and then, or sometimes I'd perfume the air with her favorite fragrance, just because it made me feel better. There were times when nothing helped, but the voice of a dear friend whose only mission was to comfort a broken heart. What I'm saying to you is that healing will happen by "trial and error," but don't stop trying. It will happen.

One minute you feel fine and in the next minute you remember every detail of your loved one's dying days. At times nothing makes sense and other times you're okay. You will find a ray of light again. Time is unstructured now. Pace yourself and allow yourself to work through your loss.

Your body, your soul and your mind will be tired. Do what you can to find peace. Do what needs to be done for your physical body, your spiritual self and your mind. In time, and with lots of love, you will emerge again, rested and ready to retake your journey.

I wish I could tell you what to do or offer you words to ease your pain, but I have come to understand that as similar as we all are, and as big as the world is, we all experience grief, sadness, tears and loss very differently when a loved one passes.

What you feel is what you feel. The truth is no one can tell you what you should do or how to feel when someone passes away. All of your feelings are normal and natural when loss comes knocking on your door. Peace, gentleness and self-care will allow you to live your new normal life. Today, I offer you my thoughts, words and loving support. Let them be part of your first step to healing.

Fourteen

A Guidebook Through Grief

Part 1 — The Grief Begins

L onging, sorrow and grief become frequent companions well before your loved one passes. With death imminent, your journey towards grief begins. Life as you understood it will change and the power of love shared during this critical time of being together will be remembered forever. As you contemplate how to be a compassionate and selfless caregiver, your loved one begins, often with fear and trepidation, a journey towards an unknown destination

Birth, unlike death, is celebrated. I did what I could to stay reverent and compassionate during my mother's last days, but caring for someone you love who is dying is exhausting. It is hard to hold onto the thoughts of joy. I wanted so much to share what I was feeling, but I was afraid to make her uncomfortable.

Then, one day she said, "Will you be okay after I'm gone?" I realized at that precise moment, as uncomfortable as it is, we all need to talk about dying and death. Mom's question began a healthy and emotional discussion about dying and death. Often we find ourselves treading lightly, especially with this issue, because we just don't know how to broach the conversation. Talking about it makes you realize that death is inevitable and our mortality is fragile.

Either the fear of losing someone holds us from revealing our innermost thoughts and feelings or we don't want to create a fortress of worry for our loved ones. We are overwhelmed by the idea of losing our dearly beloved.

I discovered that it was okay to talk about death with Mom. She gracefully opened the door with her question because she desperately needed to talk about it. She had spent much time thinking about her own mortality and then found the courage to express her deep, innermost fears. I, too, needed to talk about it.

Nearing the death of a loved one requires you to be steadfast in your faith and vigilant in your care, but what about your emotional and spiritual health? Having a conversation about dying and death, loss and grief, your fears, your loved one's fears and everything in between opens the door to a heartfelt, honest discussion that can bring you closer together.

- **Permission is granted to share your innermost feelings.**

   Mom and I spent many days talking about our family memories and how life would be for both of us after she passed. Many of us hold on to our emotions because it's hard to talk about such things. Not talking about what you're truly feeling stalls you on your journey through grief. It wasn't that Mom didn't know she was dying; she did. She needed a place that was safe to share her fears about leaving us behind and certainly about her journey beyond her death. And, it was my responsibility to allow her to share those intimate feelings even if I didn't want to admit that time was short.

You will know within your heart when it's time to talk about dying and death with your loved one. More importantly, and please trust this next statement, you will know what to say. Speak directly from your heart.

You can start by saying, *"I love you and I'm going to miss you. I know that we will always be together."*

• **Create a safe place to talk about dying and death.**

Finding the right time or the right place is never easy.

You must give your loved one and yourself an opportunity to address the deep fears about death. Taking a ride together, if possible, or sitting in the garden, or even just sitting by their bed holding hands are all places where the conversation can begin.

Mom and I sat underneath the daylight sun, smelled the fragrance of pine trees, felt the fall breezes caress our faces, and waited for a deer to appear. We decided that this was the place where we would talk. We'd spent many hours just talking about everything and nothing, both of which served us very well. Even though we were both scared, we felt better, because we did it together.

Just start by saying, *"Are you okay? If you want to talk about anything, I am here for you. I know you have a lot on your mind, but I want you to know that you don't have to go through this alone."*

- **"Honesty is the best policy."**

  Doesn't talking about what you truly feel open your heart? I think having a discussion as a family, or a conversation just between the two of you, can really promote a positive and loving exchange that will assist you during your time of grief and especially after your loved one has passed on. I sat for hours remembering the conversations I had with Mom. Knowing and hearing it first-hand that she was ready, gave me such peace at the last moments of her life.

  Having thoughtful and respectful conversations about this topic is challenging. Just be honest by saying what you feel. Let your true feelings be heard. Anything you say in a place of love will bring immeasurable healing to all who are involved.

Start by saying, *"I'm afraid, but I know my faith will keep us together forever. I'm going to miss you so much. I am so happy that we've had this time together. I love you so much."*

- **What do you do when your loved one is afraid of dying and death?**

  Without overwhelming your loved one, you spend your mornings, nights, days, and weekends doing everything you can to alleviate their fears. Simply stating "I'm here if you want to talk about what you're feeling." Just recognizing their fears opens the door to heartfelt communication, healing and the possibility of releasing fear related to death.

  Sometimes just sitting together holding hands and being silently present with each other lends itself to healing and the feeling of being supported. Sometimes words are too much. It really is your job to just be there for them as you have during every other event in their lives. Your conscious effort of loving support will guide your loved one to peace.

  Questions about life, the after-life or "Did I do enough?" or "Was I a good person?" will emerge as your loved one nears their final days.

Questions about heaven, God and "will my loved ones be there waiting for me?" may surface now and then.

During these times, just answer the questions from your understanding and truth. If you get questions that are unanswerable, just give love.

If you need the support of a Spiritual Advisor, Clergy, or Faith Counselor, seek out someone who can assist you with getting the answers that you need. Acknowledging how instrumental your loved one has been in your life will bridge anxiety to peaceful resolve.

Mom and I talked about the good days and the challenging ones, knowing that they were just days in our life together. We also recognized that our life was not measured by one singular moment, but by thousands of moments all strung together by love.

What binds us to each other is the essence of love. What holds us together long after someone has passed is remembering the love we shared.

- **Share your feelings about dying with someone.**

  It's natural to be nervous, worrisome and fearful when your loved one is dying. Talking about your fears allows for that energy to be released from your body.

  Fear causes great strife within. Talking, sharing and experiencing that fear ultimately will help to release it.

  If your loved one is not ready to have this discussion and you are, then find someone with whom you can have a serious conversation about the impending loss. Seeking out professional support or talking to a friend may be the antidote for relieving your stress. Friends are very willing to have this discussion with you because they want to help. Is there someone you can talk to right now as you're working through all of this?

- **If your loved ones are ready to share their feelings then allow them to fully engage in this conversation.**

  When Mom approached me about my being okay after she passed, I told her the truth. I was worried that the truth would hurt her. What I came to realize was that the truth opened a deep, more profound discussion about life, the after-life, her true feelings about death and my fears. By taking the opportunity to be with each other, sitting quietly and listening intently, together you'll create a time of solace, healing, and self-discovery.

I told Mom that I was afraid to be without her. My fear gave Mom a chance to hold me, to soothe me and to tell me she loved me, and in doing so, she was loved, too. She realized, as she prepared to die, that anything she needed to say was okay to say. Giving your loved ones the opportunity to share their story with you will help them walk towards their death with peace. Gently encourage them to say what they feel. If they cannot, it's okay. By sharing your feelings, this gives your loved ones permission to share theirs.

- **Talking about death is healthy.**

  Talking about death is really talking about life's entirety, because we all physically live and we all physically die. Your loved ones needs time to get their feelings in order. We spend so much time taking care of the physical body or getting our "affairs" in order. Do we take enough time to get our emotional and spiritual self in order? We seem to get stuck in the idea that our loved one is frail, but within that frailty is the essence of someone who has lived a life. Maybe they have things they want to say to you.

The human spirit is remarkable. Emotional upheavals will cause great distress to your spirit, mind and body. Having a healthy conversation about what you truly feel will open the door to a compassionate, loving moment. During this time when your loved one faces such difficult things, nothing you say, can hurt or harm. Just start loving and sharing.

- **Take care of yourself during the first step on your journey of grief.**

During the days, weeks and months prior to your loved one's passing, your life will be filled with schedules, doctor's appointments, medication adjustments, meal planning and a whole lot of errands. Even if you have a loved one in a hospital/nursing home/hospice setting, you still have the responsibility of making sure all of their needs are met and for being there for them.

So, when do you take care of yourself? Scheduling time with friends or family to sit in for you for a couple of hours is really okay to do. For you to give and to be your best, you must take time for yourself.

When my mother was dying, I didn't remember to drink water or eat meals. Others reminded me that it was important for my overall health and strength during this time. Taking naps and sleeping in now and then, were incredibly beneficial during this stage of the journey.

Doing these things will keep your body, mind and spirit strong and balanced and will support you during your grieving days. Of course, it is so hard to do this when someone you love is preparing to die. Just be as good to yourself as you are to those you love.

- **Planning moments of silence is imperative.**

  Scheduling moments of quietness and prayer during your day will help to fuel an inner strength. Whatever spiritual or religious path you choose, quiet, prayerful, reverent moments will bring you together. Remembering your faith will strengthen your reserve.

When you need time for private prayer, sitting in a church, sacred temple or in a field of luscious flowers will support you as you rebuild and refresh your energy. By finding a sacred spot for you alone (such as a park bench, by the ocean or in your car), will afford you private moments for crying, grieving and inner quieting. Taking care of your spiritual self is an important part of your healing.

- **Reach out to others for spiritual support.**

When a loved one is dying, it's okay to reach out to others for support. Friends and other family members are there to support you through this experience. The truth is, no one really knows what to say or do for you when you're grieving, so telling that person you need help is perfectly fine. That's what friends do for each other . . . they help in time of need. You are loved; so allow those who love you to give support through this experience.

Part II — A Silent Voice

Sadly, a day will come when the sound of your loved one's voice is no longer heard. The will for life dwindles day-by-day, sometimes minute-by-minute, as the condition worsens. This is the day that you must face the inevitable, that the time is upon you to say good-bye.

Mom and I spent the last two months of her life talking about dying and death, and about living and life (and somehow they were the same). We spent hours sharing our feelings, fears, and blessings that defined our lives together. We'd reminisce about the hard days and laugh about how silly some of our disagreements were. And then, we both realized how glorious the last two months had been. We embraced each other with unconditional love and understood each other on a much deeper, more compassionate level.

I remember, Friday, November 11, Mom was so full of life. Her eyes were bright, her love was vibrant and we were so glad to be together. We took pictures together, photographed our hands together and we just enjoyed each other. She lay comfortably, finally pain free, on her bed in her favorite blue smock and her smile stretched across her face to my heart. We talked about life, laughed at a few jokes and she ate her favorite ice cream. We just gazed into each other's eyes, knowing that tomorrow would never be the same. Love is such a powerful vehicle for healing. Our time together gave us a chance to gather more memories. And, then, she never spoke my name again.

As you face this day, your grief will batter you against the wall. You'll search for answers to questions that have been asked a thousand times and none will satisfy the grief that lurks within. You'll tell the doctors, please, one more day, and then, you'll call out to God because you're not ready. During this stage of grief, it is imperative to remain present for your loved one as the journey homeward begins.

- **Keep talking.**

  Keep talking even when their voices are silent. If they loved hearing your stories, they will continue to appreciate hearing your voice, long after their voice is no more. The validation needed to move through this period of your life is housed within your faith, not within the sound of your loved one's voice. I told Mom that I would never stop talking to her, no matter how hard or sad it was during her dying days. I promised to remain by her side until the very last second and beyond.

I found myself telling my Mom about the things she loved to hear about. I spoke of her departed family members by name and told her they all awaited her arrival. I shared stories of our favorite trip to New York City and offered memories of our life together. I spoke the names of her children, grandchildren and great-grandchildren, because her life was her family. I told her how much she was loved, and that our love was everlasting.

You can do that too. Your loved one will be comforted by your kindness and compassion.

Just say to them, *"I love you. I thank you and I will never forget you."*

- **You know what to do.**

  Don't waste time wondering if you're doing a good job. Haven't you always done a good job? Haven't you always given freely from your heart?

Maybe you had an emotional breakdown or you felt impatient or anxious through this experience.

We all feel discombobulated as we stand by watching our loved ones die. We waste so much time and energy worrying about what to do, when you already know what to do. When it's right, it's just right. Why not trust whatever you are being led to do for your dying loved one and continue to do it.

Your gift is your strength. Your love is a blessing. The more you recognize that within you are compassion, love and strength, the more you can accomplish for those in need.

• **St. Francis of Assisi said, "It is in giving, that we receive."**

As we give, we open the door to healing, forgiveness, letting go, and loving more deeply. It amazes me to think that when someone is dying, the dying person provides you opportunity to give of yourself. As we give, we learn something about ourselves, our strength and our willingness to stretch far beyond where we were before we began the journey. All I did from the moment Mom's voice ceased was shroud her in love. I gave her all that I had to offer and, joyfully, discovered that it was more than enough. That's all you can really do now is give. Love them with every part of your being.

- **Schedule private time for you, family and friends.**

Family, friends and old acquaintances will find their way to your loved ones bedside, offering encouragement, a collection of kisses and heart-to-heart hugs that will ease any broken heart. Many will not know what to say, but their presence and loving guidance will temporarily soothe away the grief. You'll laugh. You'll cry and you'll do what you've always done. You will love.

Plan moments to be alone with your loved one, too. These moments, by far, are the most precious moments of all. These quiet, calm, tranquil moments are times just to rest your head on their shoulders. Offer your gratitude for the wealth of life they have offered you. If you feel like combing your loved one's hair, massaging his or her hands with lotion or just sitting together, please do so. Ultimately these divinely orchestrated moments will nourish your soul long after you've said good-bye.

My memories of Mom's last days always take me back to the night I rested my head on her shoulder and stroked her arm with tenderness. I promised her that she wouldn't feel alone.

Just say, *"I am so glad your mine and I love you."*

- **Everything has a plan.**

    Sometimes, there is no more time and perhaps, you just don't have the strength or the energy to see them off to the world beyond. Time is neither short nor long; it just is what it is. The journey towards loss and grief and the death of our loved one is beyond our control.

    Please take care of yourself and do what is right for you, too. Ask for support if you feel overwhelmed. And, if you cannot do this alone, ask for help.

    You don't have to go through this alone. You don't have to sit by their bedside watching them die, if that makes you uncomfortable. You have to do what your heart tells you to do.

    This experience is like no other, so be gentle and self-nurturing during these most precious days.

- **Be present.**

  Just be present with your loved one. Being who you are and who you've always been, will shine a light deep within your loved one. Love is remembered and cannot expire. It fills the soul with awakening. Be aware and conscious of your surroundings. The awareness will allow you to feel the peaceful energy that exists beyond the suffering of loss.

- **Sit quietly.**

  Sometimes there are no more words to say. The quietness and silence is soothing for some people and not for others. By now, you've probably said everything you need to say, but if you feel that you need time to share more words, then do it now. Merged between quiet moments and conversation is something beautiful. It is your willingness to be with your loved one throughout this journey. And, that matters greatly.

  I am quite sure that our dying loved ones are working out what needs to be worked within themselves before they pass on, so all that is needed is your quiet kindness and unconditional love. As you're sitting quietly together, allow yourself to receive and give loving energy. These moments are drenched in the unconditional love you started before your loved one's voice disappeared.

• Hold hands.

Touch is soothing, nourishing and validates our existence in this world. It reminds us that we live, breathe and are one with each other. A gentle touch reminds us that we are loved and cherished. It expresses our thoughtfulness and caring. A touch tells the story of what you truly feel for the person who is dying. Being together will create a sea of love so profound that all who embrace love will feel a sense of harmony with each other.

• Say prayers together.

I read biblical passages, poems and prayers to Mom. I read from books she loved and newspaper articles I found in her dresser drawer. And, we prayed. If you believe in the power of prayer, then sharing this moment as a family or with your dying loved one will create a cohesive energy of togetherness. Sometimes, I whispered the words of Mom's favorite songs in her ear and other times I said nothing, but I love you. All of this is prayer.

- **Get help. You deserve it.**

  As you gingerly walk through this stage of loss, your dying loved is blessed by your comforting kindness. Let's face it; this is hard stuff to deal with. During this phase of grief, searching for support from those who are willing to help will fuel moments of sanity. There is no doubt that what you feel is beyond colossal.

  Asking for support will help you walk through your personal process. Walking through grief at all stages, versus walking around it will benefit your overall wellness during the experience of loss, grief and bereavement.

  This is painful no matter who you are, so take time and be patient and ask for help.

- **It's okay to cry.**

  Crying says that you are human. Crying is giving your body, your soul and your emotions a chance to release pain. Crying is a strength not a weakness or a frailty in your composition. I allowed myself to cry in front of my mother because that was my truth. I was sad. Family and friends cry together and get through each minute, together. We celebrate, we rejoice, we mourn and we remember. We all stood at this doorway, hand-to-hand, heart-to-heart.

Your sadness does not define you. The love that you shared will rise above the grief when time has moved forward.

Part III — After the Loss

Grief is uniquely personal. It's a process of occurrences that escalates your emotions after the loss of a loved one. Your life becomes filled with disbelief, brokenness, anger, longing, suffering, sadness and a whole lot of uncomfortable feelings and experiences.

Somehow, through the mystery of it all, acceptance emerges where your strength and faith meet. As universal as grief is, each person walks through the stages of grief at their own pace, own time and sometimes out of sequence.

According to the Kubler-Ross model of grief, there are five stages: denial, anger, depression, bargaining, and acceptance. Grief as we know it is experienced multiple times during the trials and tribulations of our lives. The stages of grief offer a different set of emotional, mental, physical, and spiritual consequences as a result of the loss.

The best thing that you can do is tackle each emotion and experience as it comes.

- **You now have permission to shed your armor and your tears.**

    We often find ourselves crying silently during our initial time of grief. You have many thoughts and feelings rummaging around in your mind. Your heart feels so heavy. Questions bombard your thoughts and peace seems nowhere to be found. Often you say to yourself "Did I do enough?" or "Did I give enough of myself?"

    Remembering how you cared for and loved your departed loved one, matters. Whatever you gave to the one in need, if given from a place of truth, unconditional love and selflessness, then you gave everything you could. By giving of yourself, you created an opening for healing, for yourself, your family and for the one you miss.

Tears are natural and a normal reaction to such a traumatic change in one's life. Crying on the shoulder of friend is healthy and healing. Is there someone you can call right now to support you as you grieve?

Often, I found myself saying to my family and friends, "I want to talk to you about what I'm feeling, but I don't want you to say anything right now. Is that okay?" They love you, so they will oblige you with unconditional support.

Trust what you are feeling and if you are so overwhelmed, then ask for help.

Just start by saying, *"I need you right now or I need to talk right now."*

- **It's true: everything has changed.**

  The idea of losing a loved one, someone that you have shared a life with, now gone, creates immeasurable pain. Pain becomes a blockage of life.

  Often, as grief stricken souls, we avoid addressing the effects of denial and pain because grief is too intense and we are in a form of shock. Denial is harsh and, if left untreated, can have lasting effects on your life. What will make you stronger over time is the idea that you did, in fact, share love. It's true, it all looks different now, but you will find the essence of love that the two of you shared.

- **Grief has no expiration date.**

  What may be helpful during your time of grief is actively getting the pain out of the body. By talking to friends and family, immediately after your loss, you will begin to move this heaviness out of you.

  Please remember that you will have this feeling, many days, months or even years, after your loved one passes. As I am sharing these words with you, it is exactly sixteen months since Mom's passing.

  As we navigate the road to our new normal way of living, there will be triggers: songs, stories, pictures and lots of other things that will cause you to feel the energy of loss again. Simply, gently, lovingly walk through that moment knowing that your dearly beloved surrounds you with the same loving compassion that you gave them.

- **Release guilt.**

  I felt guilt for thinking that I didn't do enough. After repeated meditations, I know in my heart it was enough and I gave all that I could. Often when I drive home from a distance, I find myself traveling different routes, roadways and highways back to my house. There's more than one way to get home, back to where you belong.

  So it is with grief. There are many ways to walk towards releasing guilt and rediscovering the healing. Do what you can to take of yourself at this moment. What I found most interesting during the experience of grief was that I visited many of the stages of grief more than once and at different times. I've come to understand that this is a normal part of grieving.

- **Remember forgiveness.**

  As you maneuver through this unanticipated journey, you will be consumed by your grief. Stop and just be in a space of love. Remembering the love you shared, the words exchanged and the forgiveness, opens the door to a new pathway. Forgiveness is simply choosing to no longer be held by old energies and experiences. Forgiveness fuels and fosters ease within your soul.

- **Okay, you're angry! This is normal when you're grieving.**

  Anger is one of those emotions that creep up when you least expect it. It's true you're trying to adjust to a new way of living, without the one who's passed away. Anger creates a wave of unsettled energy that disturbs your mind, body and spirit.

  I took walks up and down the driveway to exert that energy I was feeling. I took long drives to work out my pain. Often, I wrote little notes in a journal to address the emotional upheaval that I felt.

  I found that addressing my anger immediately was necessary for me to keep walking forward. I noticed that every time I addressed the anger versus not paying attention to it, the anger diminished until it was gone. I realized that as I reconnected to the loving memories of my loved one, I felt strong again.

- **What is required now is nothing but self-love.**

  You'll find that you can breathe a little easier by sharing your feelings, sorrow, regrets and all that comes when someone you love dies. Finding a place to rest your head, a refuge of sorts, can be spiritually nurturing during your difficult time of loss. Sitting in a church, in a field of flowers, gazing into the sky or just being present with what you feel, can help to restore you.

I quickly figured out that hugs and the compassion bestowed by others was incredibly therapeutic during the most acute times of denial, pain, disbelief and sadness. So, allowing others to help can be beneficial in the healing process. Sometimes, we think that we have to handle it all by ourselves, but this is not the case.

Seek out help, get support, and allow yourself the appropriate time you need to work through this life-altering experience.

- **Separation from your loved one exists in your mind only.**

The heart knows what it knows. Faith allows us to believe that beyond the doorway to death is life in a golden place. When I was distracted, fearful and overwhelmed, I realigned with my belief that no matter what we will always be together.

- **You have permission to breath, laugh and live again.**

  Finding ways to breathe through your emotions is vital. Remembering to laugh again is crucial. In my years of channeling messages, I never heard or felt a spirit say "be sad." I believe they want us to live on, joyfully, finding our way back to who we are. We forget to breathe, laugh and live when loss consumes our world.

  I did the "Sixty Second Spiritual Workout" to regain my inner composure. I would consciously breathe for sixty seconds: count to sixty in my head and breathe deeply. This exercise alleviated my suffering and allowed my inner light to shine.

  Every time you find yourself holding your breath, try readjusting your awareness and concentration on your breath. It may not take your grief away, but it makes the journey a little easier.

- **Simply keep reminding yourself, that what you feel is what you feel.**

  Here are a few things to do when grief and loss hold you hostage: be kind to yourself, plan moments of quietness, address your anger or emotions and speak to someone if you need help.

  It is important to walk through your grief, not around it. Grief will always be there, but to what measure will it consume your daily life? What are some of the things you can do right now to get yourself to feel peaceful? In the midst of darkness, what are some of the things you can do to see the light again?

  There is no "cure-all" for grief. It is what it is and you can only do your best. In time, hope will be restored and until then recognize that what you feel is what you feel.

- **Remember the memories.**

  Memories are enveloped by the love that we've shared in our lifetime with each other and remain a part of our soul's evolution. Holding those memories within our hearts will give us strength again. Certainly, in the beginning of our expedition into grief, the memories can overwhelm us. When the time is right after addressing the denial and pain, memories will become a peaceful refuge for healing.

- **Love is the greatest communicator between God, Spirit, our dearly beloveds, and mankind.**

  Beyond the grief, lies the image of their faces, the essence of who they were to us in life and the love they imparted to us.

  Love has been and will always be the greatest spiritual communicator between God and man. There is no cliché too powerful for what love is and how it can change us. Every cell in our human body and every aspect of our humanness understand the truth about love.

  I know that when the dark days come, sitting back, connecting in the heart, visualizing the images of love, I will, we all will, be restored.

  Love is everlasting. Love is forever. Love is eternal.

16 Minutes
When One Breath Ends, Another Begins
Grief Support Teleconference
with Roland M. Comtois

If you're at a standstill with grief and you feel alone, please know that I am here to help.

Join me for a heartfelt, warm, and honest conversation about dying, death, loss, the after-life, and grief.

Together, we will walk, slowly and steadily through the experience of grief. We will stretch our hearts to each other and realize that we are truly not alone on this journey.

As a purchaser of my book, you are invited to attend this yearly teleconference and join the conversation.

Simply scan the QR Code on the previous page or go to:

http://www.BlessingsByRoland.com/
16minutes_teleconference

About Roland M. Comtois

A sought-after TV and radio personality, channel, and best-selling lecturer whose personal appearances and "Channeled Messages for the Soul" presentations take him throughout the United States and Europe, Roland has earned a devoted following. Hundreds of thousands of clients from all over the world, of all ages, and from all walks of life who regularly seek his spiritual counsel during healing sessions, special events, group workshops, and book signings.

Roland is the author of two books: *And Then There Was Heaven, A Journey of Hope and Love*, and *16*

Minutes, A Guidebook for Grief. He is working on his third book, *The Purple Papers*, which documents the stories behind his amazing purple paper messages, as well as a television show by the same name.

Visit http://www.BlessingsbyRoland.com for more.

Other Titles from Roland

And Then There Was Heaven
A Journey of Hope and Love
Published in 2009

Roland's first book showcases the acclaimed channeler's own real life experiences, messages, and truths about love, life, and heaven in an engaging and personal narrative that is unlike any book on the subject.

In doing so, he takes you to the bedsides of those who are about to cross over, to the hearts of those who have lost a loved one, to the reunions of those he reunites in spirit.

But then he goes one step further, venturing beyond the veil to share his own journey up the brilliant staircase, and back down to earth again where he continues to impart the message that love is eternal and never, ever, dies.

This book promises to be a captivating read, containing within priceless nuggets of comfort, hope, wisdom and advice you can turn to as you through your own life's journey. It's like accessing secrets for the soul that have the power to manifest all the spiritual abundance and healing that Roland feels every day and making them a part of your own.

Silent Night . . . The Meditation
Published in 2012

This is Roland's first vocal performance, which was released on 12-31-2012. Roland will take you on a spiritual, reverent, and meditative journey, along with Steven Antonio Lupo (Producer/Arranger) that will open your heart. With the sound and gentleness of Tibetan bells, piano, acoustic guitar, and angelic voices, you will feel peace, love, and will rest quietly in the arms of the angels.

Spiritual Communications: Messages, Mediums & Mysteries
Published in 2013

This 2-1/2 hour, 2-disk set, is Roland's first teaching CD about Spiritual Communication. Roland says that "every human being has the ability to communicate with God, Spirit, Angels, and Loved Ones." Simply by quieting your mind and easing your tension, the opportunity to receive divine messages will be found.

Sit back, relax and let Roland take you on a journey of inspiration, teachings and love.

Love is Eternal.

For more information about Roland or to purchase the products above, visit his website at:

www.BlessingsByRoland.com

New Titles Coming in 2013–2014

A Date with Destiny
Near Death Moments, Life-Changing Lessons

– and –

The Purple Papers ... And The Stories Behind Them